♈♉♊♋

MANIF̶ ̶̶ION
THROUGH
ZODIAC SIGNS

♈♉♊♋♌♍♎♏♐♑♒♓

How they manipulate you and how you
can protect yourself from it

by Alex Lakraft

What motivates the author…

Since the dramatic misuse of recently discovered astrological knowledge has continued to gain momentum, I seek to warn and protect people against the severe risks posed by rampant tampering.

I have experienced a lot of pain as a result of the manipulative practices used against me and others by a woman who used to be a very good friend of mine. She was thus always able to get the best result for herself and take real advantage of others. Fortunately, I uncovered her dark secret and have published this book so that people can use this knowledge to defend themselves. Because I well remember how unsuspecting and helpless I once was. These practices are painful attacks on the human psyche!

On Facebook:
https://www.facebook.com/
ManipulationThroughZodiacSigns

On Twitter:
https://twitter.com/AlexLakraft

E-mail:
contactlakraft@gmail.com

Alex Lakraft

Table of Contents

Preface

Dear reader,

Manipulation according to zodiac signs, doesn't that sound a little extreme? Could it really be possible to consciously manipulate another person with the help of their zodiac sign? I didn't want to believe this either when I suddenly became an accidental witness of how accessible our zodiac signs make us to unconscious influences – or even conscious manipulation – through people of other zodiac signs. I noticed this when I was able to observe how a friend of mine repeatedly managed to get access to advantages and benefits that were actually contrary to the other person's interest when in contact with them. Apparently, she always managed to create the best situation possible for herself and thereby literally overtook others. Since she had not been successful at all for a long time in her life, this was even more remarkable. Her career was not going well and her relationships were also failing. However, from one day to the other, her life completely changed. She was able to celebrate professional success and could not save herself from all her admirers. This turn made me curious but at the same time, I observed her behavior with suspicion and certain disapproval. Manipulating other people cannot be justified by anything. For this reason, I hope that you, dear readers, will not use the information in this book, which will undoubtedly change your life just like it changed my friend's life, either to unscrupulously manipulate others. It should only make you able to protect yourself from the influence and manipulation due to your zodiac sign.

But back to my friend: Through persistent research I found out that she had acquired astrological knowledge that enabled her to influence any person according to their zodiac sign and use it to her advantage. You can imagine how much this realization shocked me. If my friend was able to manipulate someone like that without people who didn't know her as well as me noticing, then how often had I been a victim of this kind of manipulation? I started to delve into this topic and came across simple as well as astonishing connections that I don't want to keep from you.

The book shows how people manipulate each other according to their zodiac signs and how one can protect oneself from it. Thereby it is all about knowledge that is very simple, but cannot be acquired by all astrologist naturally, because this simple knowledge can only be drawn indirectly from astrological books. One simply gets it when thinking about it. I dedicate this book to this very knowledge in order to warn and protect people from manipulative dangers.

Chapter I is about the mutual influences of people of the same and different zodiac signs. Thereby it is crucial which position the respective zodiac sign has to your own position in the zodiac scheme, e.g. next to it, across from it or somewhere else.

Chapter II talks in detail about the manipulative competencies of each zodiac sign, e.g. which powers a person with the zodiac sign Aries has and why.

Chapter III is dedicated to perhaps the most touchy subject: The information on how to manipulate another person with the help of their zodiac sign.

I. The mutual influence of the zodiac signs

Observing the stars of our solar system probably dates back to the start of humanity itself. The cradle of modern astrology lies in the old Babylon, so more than 2,500 years ago. Since then the knowledge of the influence of the zodiac signs of personality and destiny has constantly been enlarged and handed down by other cultures. The great astronomers of the Middle Ages such as Johannes Kepler were also passionate astrologers at the same time. In the past years, various scientific studies have shown that astrology is not just an esoteric invention but rather handed-down knowledge with a scientific origin.

Here it is important to know that not only the date and time of our birth influence our personality and course of life, but that we are influenced in various ways by the effects of the stars of our solar system throughout our entire life. For every zodiac sign is assigned to a different star dominating over it, for example, Mars dominates over Aries, Jupiter dominates over Sagittarius, etc. Besides the 12 signs of the zodiac, there are the 12 houses that correspond to the zodiac signs throughout the year. The sixth house, for example, stands under the influence of the zodiac sign Virgo. Here it is all about orderliness, talent for organizing, willingness to serve and scientific talent. At the same time, the 12 houses also stand for the individual stages of life that we go through and in which we change and grow due to our experiences. So far the mutual influences that people with different or the same zodiac signs have on each other have only been observed insufficiently. When looking for a partner it has long been said that certain zodiac signs are only limitedly suitable for a relationship together due to their characteristics, while others match perfectly. The versatile Gemini and the ambitious Capricorn, for example, only rarely make a good couple, unless they find a way to complement each other. Certain zodiac signs attract each other while others push each other away.

This book is primarily about showing that our zodiac signs do not only play an important role when picking a partner but that they influence us on a daily basis when interacting with others. There are friends, relatives and colleagues but also random acquaintances such as a doctor's visit or grocery shopping. The power of the stars of our solar system is always present, even if we can't consciously perceive it. But if we become aware of it, we are able to, for one, notice how zodiac signs influence our allegedly free decisions and we notice when someone tries to manipulate us in this manner. You will be surprised how simple it is to understand this knowledge and implement it in everyday life. You, just like me, will probably ask yourself why you didn't realize it on your own, but due to the experiences of my friend, I can assure you that this knowledge already exists and is being used. Only a conscious analysis can keep it from being a disadvantage for you.

The secret types of manipulation

A basic rule is that there are 12 different types of manipulation for each member of one of the 12 zodiac signs. Each type depends on the individual relationship between people. The role of the manipulator and the person that is to be manipulated can change hereby because these manipulations take place unconsciously most of the time. Each zodiac sign influences us subliminally in its own way, not always with a manipulative objective, but it changes our perception and our mood.

In case one zodiac sign has clear intentions to influence you, they are always of manipulative character and are also expressed towards your zodiac sign according to their respective sign. Of course, you don't always have to suspect bad intentions of all people around you. But manipulations are part of everyday life and therefore it is recommended to always stay alert to a reasonable degree. The special danger

13

of zodiac sign-related manipulation is the fact that all people have already built-in instinctive mechanisms that enable them to find out the personality type of a person completely unconsciously and subsequently shape a certain manipulative attitude and behavior towards this person. This means that our tendency to react to all zodiac signs is already instinctively programmed in us. That is why the tendencies of how a contact between people of certain zodiac signs will develop are generally known. Not every influence by another sign of the zodiac is of negative or manipulative nature. On the contrary, we can further develop and receive important impulses through the conscious perception of the influences of other zodiac signs. Depending which phase of life we are in and what we are internally working on, meeting people of a certain zodiac sign can help us gain understanding and inner maturity as well as help us overcome problems. Meeting a person from the same zodiac sign, for example, lets us better recognize our own strengths so that we are able to assert ourselves and prevail more easily.

The 12 zodiac signs are assigned to the 12 periods in which the sun moves. This way the sun travels through these three signs in spring: Aries, Taurus and Gemini. In summer, it travels through the next three signs: Cancer, Leo and Virgo. Afterwards Libra, Scorpio and Sagittarius follow in fall. In winter, the cycle closes with the last three signs: Capricorn,

Aquarius and Pisces. To each zodiac sign, a symbol has been assigned.

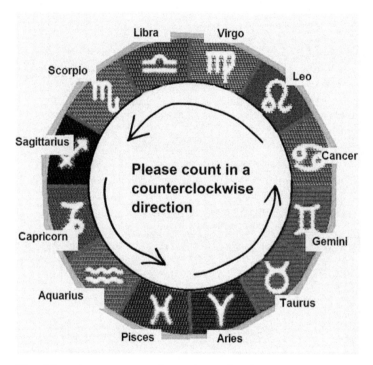

The 12 zodiac signs in the zodiac wheel

In the image one can clearly see that each zodiac sign does not only have two neighbors, but also one directly across from them. These positions are crucial for the mutual influence and manipulation.

The periods of the sun in the 12 signs of the zodiac:

Sign	Period	Sign	Period
Aries	March 21st – April 20th	**Libra**	September 23rd – October 22nd
Taurus	April 21st – May 21st	**Scorpio**	October 23rd – November 22nd
Gemini	May 22nd – June 21st	**Sagittarius**	November 23rd – December 20th
Cancer	June 22nd – July 22nd	**Capricorn**	December 21st – January 19th
Leo	July 23rd – August 22nd	**Aquarius**	January 20th – February 18th
Virgo	August 23rd – September 22nd	**Pisces**	February 19th – March 20th

The 12 zodiac signs are grouped into 4 essential elements:

Fire	Aries	Leo	Sagittarius
Earth	Taurus	Virgo	Capricorn
Air	Gemini	Libra	Aquarius
Water	Cancer	Scorpio	Pisces

1st topic "self-perception": You and people of the same zodiac sign

It is a matter of one of the following connections:

You	Your opponent
Aries	Aries
Taurus	Taurus
Gemini	Gemini
Cancer	Cancer
Leo	Leo
Virgo	Virgo
Libra	Libra
Scorpio	Scorpio
Sagittarius	Sagittarius
Capricorn	Capricorn
Aquarius	Aquarius
Pisces	Pisces

First, we will talk about the mutual interaction with and possible manipulation through a person of the same zodiac sign.

Oftentimes, we can recognize ourselves in people of the same zodiac signs. We can relate to their actions and values and have mutual goals and preferences. Initially, this sounds as if we could neither learn a lot from a person of the same zodiac sign nor be manipulated by them, but that is not correct. Meeting a person of the same zodiac sign can help us better recognize and use our strengths. Through them, we learn how we can assert ourselves in the world and how to trust in ourselves.

A person of the same zodiac sign is our mirror and therefore puts us in a position to get to know ourselves. A carrier of the same zodiac sign stimulates you to think about your own personality due to his own behavior. That way, you discover your mental habits and character traits that help you advance in life and at the same time you also get to know the characteristics and traits of the psyche that keep you from fully scooping out your potential. Those are the positive influences that we experience from people of the same zodiac sign. So if you are in a phase of self-doubt and fear of the future, the positive and conscious encounter with a person of the same sign can help you solve these problems and strengthen yourself.

At best, such a collaboration, friendship or partnership is about a fair, equal contact without a clear superiority on one of the two sides.

Such connections can potentially be destructive because when our will is considerably stimulated, the more often we are in contact with people of our first sign. Although such stimuli, that help strengthen our self-confidence, are usually good and desirable, such a transformative trend can slowly become unhealthy and go beyond all borders, eventually ending in a stubborn self-will and brutal selfishness. It is to be stressed that the developments will proceed in accordance with the respective zodiac sign. This means that the positive as well as the negative aspects of an existing zodiac sign will intensify in this case. When in constant contact with our mirror sign, we create a small, careless world fit for our interests for each other that can be very one-sided and that always moves in the same direction. One can very well imagine which dimensions these processes can amount to and how much these people can motivate and manipulate each other.

The familiarity of the people of the same sign also has its pitfalls when we observe in which ways it can manipulate us. Manipulation coming from people of your first sign, how we call the same sign, are hard to identify as such, because everything in connection with this person seems familiar and right. Just like we don't mistrust ourselves, we also don't mistrust people with the same sign of the zodiac.

The interaction with these people is connected to the magic of naturalness, one pretty much understands each other without words. But this is exactly what is dangerous. During these encounters, we are gladly willing to drop any caution and to listen to our impulses. This is exactly what a counterpart that wants to manipulate us will use to its advantage.

In order for you to protect yourself against manipulation when in contact with your own sign, you must learn to control your will. Discipline of the will and self-control form the most important principle which you need to pay attention to when dealing with the people of your first sign. We must avoid this temptation to be busy with ourselves in a naive and easy manner and to enforce our interests and needs in an especially ruthless way. A very egocentric lifestyle can be the result, since one's own behavior is no longer questioned by alternative lifestyles, but only confirmed by the people of the same sign. If, all of a sudden, you find yourself feeling as if you have no chance anymore to put a stop to negative self-development, you create a certain distance to this person, in order to weaken this development. Why do these processes occur? The reason for this is that two people of the same sign come into resonance with each other. The energy structure that this sign possesses becomes denser and therefore all characteristics of the affected sign are intensified. An intensified desire of both people of the same zodiac sign that can be described with the words "simply be yourself" can indeed make sense to a certain degree, but furthermore abruptly lead to a trap of ignorant self-satisfaction. Nobody will understand you quite like a person of the same sign, because you get each other pretty easily in this connection and all mutual flaws, habits and inabilities are very familiar to both. Watch out! Such a person often makes you see what you want to see. This circumstance paves the way for manipulation. The carrier of our sign, by the way, can be manipulated by us to the same extent and maybe you have already done this, without being aware of the mechanisms.

Sometimes the relationships between people of the same sign develop into a type of competition that can apply to any area of life, both in business as well as in love relationships or friendships. In this case, you should ask yourself whether you really want to get stuck in an ongoing routine; whether consciously or unconsciously, you can feel forced to play games of rivalry and competition. Here a piece of advice would be appropriate: Don't give in to these provocative games, because it is not about outdoing your mirror sign, but rather about optimally managing everyday life, effectively solving certain tasks and to properly work on your goals. Keep a cool head and don't let yourself be provoked by every person that wants to push their ego-based rivalry onto you. Rather compete with the people around you instead of your mirror sign.

2nd topic "material values": You and people of your second sign

This involves one of the following associations:

You	Your opponent
Aries	Taurus
Taurus	Gemini
Gemini	Cancer
Cancer	Leo
Leo	Virgo
Virgo	Libra
Libra	Scorpio
Scorpio	Sagittarius
Sagittarius	Capricorn
Capricorn	Aquarius
Aquarius	Pisces
Pisces	Aries

After having looked at the mutual influence of people of the same sign, we will now have a look at the mutual influence and possible manipulation of you and the zodiac sign that is right next to you in the zodiac.

The manipulative power of the so-called second sign towards you is usually estimated not to be that strong. But it is rather the other way around. You have a clear manipulative superiority over your second sign, because you play the role of the 12th sign in this connection. In order to gain your trust, a person of your second sign will shower you with various gifts, benefits and money. A person like this will often also try to seduce you in a sexual way. In order to wrap you around their finger, the second sign will work on giving you a feeling of security and comfort of material overflow. So watch out that you do not lose your vigilance due to all the comfort and care that a person of the second sign could give you. Also, they tend to memorize many thoughts and statements that you express, because the accumulated information about you can be used effectively for manipulative purposes. Not seldom, the second sign behaves in a way as if it would like to keep you away from anything dangerous and at this, gains more and more influence on you. Don't let such a person get in between you and your environment and put them in their place on time. Don't give away the control over your life! You always have to be in control of the most important strings. You have to make the biggest decisions that determine your life, and nobody else!

Otherwise, the people of your second sign can be of great use to you. You can get a lot from them, not only material-wise. By nature, a person of the second sign can recognize your qualities and talents very well and help you promote them. They can also provide you with material support.

The contact with your second sign stimulates you to think about materiel and spiritual values. How can one make the most use of everything you own? How do you manage your possessions in a way that it improves your life and the life of your relatives most effectively? Are you satisfied with your income and how can you influence it? How do you invest your savings, if at all? Which talents, characteristics and competencies you possess are you already aware of and what is there to discover? The most important feed for thought that contact with your second sign gives you is: What is valuable to you? What do you value most and what is rather not important to you? Optimize the balance between material and spiritual values according to your liking. Don't let anyone talk you into something here, because your life with all its decisions belongs only to you and nobody else.

3rd topic "communication": You and people of your third sign

Thereby it is a matter of one of the following connections:

You	Your opponent
Aries	Gemini
Taurus	Cancer
Gemini	Leo
Cancer	Virgo
Leo	Libra
Virgo	Scorpio
Libra	Sagittarius
Scorpio	Capricorn
Sagittarius	Aquarius
Capricorn	Pisces
Aquarius	Aries
Pisces	Taurus

We are moving forward in the circle of the zodiac signs and will have a look at the third sign now. Communication is everything in life. Consciously or unconsciously, we are in constant exchange with our fellow human beings, verbally as well as non-verbally. Through communication, we create our environment: work place, friendships and partnerships. People of the third sign have a great manipulative effect on us. They can influence us through our personal environment by controlling communication. It is important to know that there is no such thing as neutral communication. It is always attached to opinions, individual experiences, the cultural and social context and even ideologies. There are true masters of communication that manage to consciously manipulate the opinion of people around them with the help of subtle means in language, gestures and other communication.

Communication is the level on which we deal with people of the third sign and oftentimes they are better at it. Sometimes they even manage to change our environment to a certain degree by showing us the truth about the attitudes and opinions of the people around us. This can be very positive for us because that way we can realize who is really good for us and who is not. We can better decide with who's views we agree and recognize if someone is honest to us or is manipulating us through shaping opinions, for example through rumors. But the influence of the third sign goes even further:

People of the third sign stimulate you to leave the well-trodden paths of thinking and to get excited about new areas of interest. You are intellectually challenged and grow. Your third sign will also teach you how to effectively develop and to make your intelligence usable, in order to properly use it for the sake of the community. If consciously or not, these people give you certain impulses that help you to bring your own analytical and logical thinking to a new level. These people give you numerous possibilities of all kind that enable you to learn something new and hear about current information in general, so that you can keep yourself up to date. The knowledge that they give you is mostly not only oriented towards your areas of interest, but also those of your environment, which turns out to be very helpful and handy to you, because it contributes to your general knowledge in many ways. And the most important thing that the third sign can teach you is the ability to flexibly and quickly adapt to the constantly changing circumstances in your environment.

When in contact with the people of our third sign we are not always moving in the same direction like we do often do when in contact with our first sign. Also be warned that these people are able to choose their words and statements very skillfully to their advantage. And again you can learn from them, because you will definitely learn how to use all situations, even complicated ones, in your environment to your advantage from the approach of your third sign. Such friendships have the potential to reach a brotherly level. Such a partnership is also very good for business. Friends and work colleagues of your third sign are often situated in other cities or even abroad. They slowly tend to develop a healthy amount of curiosity and respect towards you. By the way, it is also recommended to take good care of contacts with people of your third sign, because almost no other sign can contribute so much to your mental strength. With no other sign, you can have such a limitlessly informative exchange so quickly.

The third sign has so many positive things in store for you. But what about manipulation? In connection with the topic communication, it is important to always keep in mind that there is almost no such thing as unconscious influence. Communication always takes place consciously and is therefore an appropriate tool of manipulation. One of the possibilities is to make us change our beliefs and ideologies. All of a sudden, we find arguments that we always used to reject convincing and change our views.

But how does a person of the third sign of the zodiac after our own manage to manipulate us? Friendships are often successfully developed and the third sign usually reaches out to you for joint activities, spending time and going on trips. It isolates you from other contacts and gives you the feeling of being intellectually superior to your previous friends, so that you are no longer accessible for their views. A person of the third sign can make you question everything that you think you know about yourself through well-placed remarks about other people, your look and your lifestyle. This manipulation can lead to you being tempted to do things that you actually don't like. And the influence goes even further: The third sign can literally tempt you to run after damaging opinions and ideologies that can acquire characteristics of a cult. The best protection from such manipulation is not to let yourself be isolated. Remain open for communication and the views of others and trust in what old friends and close relatives tell you when you start changing your views and lifestyle under the influence of someone from the third sign.

4th topic "tradition": You and persons of your fourth sign

This involves one of the following associations:

You	Your opponent
Aries	Cancer
Taurus	Leo
Gemini	Virgo
Cancer	Libra
Leo	Scorpio
Virgo	Sagittarius
Libra	Capricorn
Scorpio	Aquarius
Sagittarius	Pisces
Capricorn	Aries
Aquarius	Taurus
Pisces	Gemini

In this section, we deal with the influence and possible manipulation by a person of the fourth sign. We encounter the fourth sign at the level of traditions and values, which have been anchored in our subconscious as a result of our upbringing. We hold on to our traditions because they give us security, we no longer actively question them, while dissociating from them is a difficult process. Since we experienced them as children, they have long since become second nature to us and – in most cases – we actually seek to pass them on to our own children. We shall deal with the fourth sign not on an intellectual but an emotional level.

We often recognize persons of the fourth sign by them being willing to offer us advice – advice which, in fact, not uncommonly turns out to be useful. Sometimes, though, this advice is of a manipulative character. The fourth sign will attempt to exert influence on you by, say, offering you all kinds of support and aid. No effort is spared in maintaining a harmonious and peaceful relationship with you. In the course of discussions with you, these persons attempt to provide you with a feeling of stability and conformity – which can have an effect on you similar to a calming drug. By this means, they appeal to your conscience, morals and traditions. When in contact with your fourth sign, you can constantly feel a whiff of smugness.

The fourth sign is keen on talking to you about your past, thereby learning a lot about you. On the basis of intuitive inspiration, these persons are able to test the truthfulness of your information. At the mental level, contact with persons of your fourth sign enables you to think about how much value you attach to stability and security in your life. The question arises whether you can readily accept uncertainty or whether clarity is ultimately of great importance for you, whether it is easy for you to resign yourself to an uprooted life or whether familiarity and a precise overview suits you better.

In spite of all the beneficial influences, there is a danger of your fourth sign exerting a restrictive effect on you, thereby restraining you from undergoing the change you need from time to time. By this means, a superfluous paternalism and an overbearing care are imposed on you, which could appreciably adversely affect your potential for development. In major problem situations, such as the death of a close relative or divorce, contact with a person of the fourth sign can provide us with security and act as a kind of moral compass, so that we do not lose our way. Persons of the fourth sign are ideally suited as a business partner, since we share the same discourse on values with them.

The great danger in encountering a fourth sign is if it results in us no longer challenging the values handed down to us, thereby denying us inner development and external progress. Although traditions are certainly important, so too is change. The fourth sign manipulates us by appealing to our identity that we feel, to our desire for belonging and a home, and makes us fearful of becoming outcast and criticized. An integral component of a happy life consists of being able to question and reject the values of our parents while developing our own. In order to protect ourselves from manipulation by the fourth sign, it is important that we do not allow ourselves to be lulled by what seems familiar and therefore right to us but instead remain receptive to changes.

5th topic "creative self-expression": You and persons of your fifth sign

Thereby it is a matter of one of the following connections:

You	Your opponent
Aries	Leo
Taurus	Virgo
Gemini	Libra
Cancer	Scorpio
Leo	Sagittarius
Virgo	Capricorn
Libra	Aquarius
Scorpio	Pisces
Sagittarius	Aries
Capricorn	Taurus
Aquarius	Gemini
Pisces	Cancer

We now come to the fifth sign – as seen from your zodiac sign. Persons of your fifth sign are characterized by the fact that you encounter them in a context of pleasure, celebrating, parties, hobbies and similar interests. They have an almost intoxicating effect on you. They stimulate your creativity, fire your imagination and inspire you to launch new projects. In the presence of the fifth sign, you get to know new people and have the feeling of absolutely brimming over with new ideas. Life is transformed into a party and pleasure plays an important role. We have an urgent desire to express ourselves and come into contact with others. We are eager to try out new things and embark on adventures.

In the presence of persons of the fifth sign, we often feel alive and well in a new and unfamiliar way. It is easy to identify the positive aspects of this influence: we become inspired, gain new impressions and find ways of expressing ourselves.

Persons of the fifth sign provide you with entertainment and fun, which may well assume manipulative features. The fifth sign keeps you in a good mood and you rarely experience boredom with it. These persons bring out the inner child in you in an amusing and playful manner. They often stage pepped-up appearances for you. You are presented with fun, joyful attitude and optimism before your very eyes. In time, contact with these persons gives you the knack of being able to express yourself effectively and precisely. You have the feeling as if a different, better you were emerging through contact with the fifth sign.

Your fifth sign can inspire you to new ideas, and enthuse you to embark on new beginnings and projects. Nevertheless, you should take the ecstasy associated with this encounter with a grain of salt. Persons of the fifth sign often behave in fickle and insincere manner. They are willing to share the good times with us, but not the bad times. As soon as the party is over, they cast us off and move on, frequently leaving us with an emotional hangover.

The problem with your fifth sign can also be that these persons often pretend and show off. They are rarely what they seem at first sight. In other words, they like to act out roles so as not to show themselves as they really are. Persons of the fifth sign manipulate us by making us literally addicted to their presence. They make us believe that we need them in order to feel alive and creative. This can lead to an emotional dependency and even to abuse. This is because – alongside the glittering world of art and parties – the fifth sign is also familiar with the aspects of unpredictability and emotional cruelty. Persons of the fifth sign need you as their counterpart to provide more credibility to their own illusory world. In this regard, your admiration is the nectar that sustains them. The encounter with your fifth sign can inspire and motivate you. If you are urgently searching for new impulses and a radical change in your life, then these are the persons for you. The great risk here is that you lose yourself in them and undergo a change of character without actually noticing. Do not allow yourself to be blinded by them but remain true to yourself – this is the most important piece of advice you can be given in this context.

6th topic "submission": You and persons of your sixth sign

This involves one of the following associations:

You	Your opponent
Aries	Virgo
Taurus	Libra
Gemini	Scorpio
Cancer	Sagittarius
Leo	Capricorn
Virgo	Aquarius
Libra	Pisces
Scorpio	Aries
Sagittarius	Taurus
Capricorn	Gemini
Aquarius	Cancer
Pisces	Leo

We now encounter your sixth sign of the zodiac. Contact with our sixth sign involves the subjects of "service", "habit", "compromise" and "daily routine". Here, however, you have less to worry about: in this case, you are the one with the manipulative potential – yours is much stronger than your counterpart. This means that you can relatively easily dominate and intimidate your sixth sign. Even if you can't help it and do your very best to treat these persons with velvet gloves, it nevertheless often happens that you exercise a destructive effect on them. These persons tend to come out on the losing side of practically every conflict and argument with you.

The possibilities for manipulation on the part of your sixth sign result from its perseverance in exercising a permanent influence on you. These persons feel a strong attraction to you and are willing to perform all kinds of favours and services for you. You should show particular consideration when interacting with persons of your sixth sign, as they might easily become afraid of you due their different character structure. Thoughtfulness and helpfulness are important lessons that you can learn from your sixth sign. First and foremost, it is a question of accommodating yourself to your sixth sign's daily routine. As a rule, what is appreciated here is specific and precise knowledge, skills and clear ways of thinking that are effectively applied in practice.

A large number of contacts with persons of your sixth sign result in their influences on you causing changes to the principles and schemes, according to which you govern and organize your daily life. By this means, you acquire new habits, rethink how you deal with your health, adopt a different attitude to work, correct your perception of your immediate environment, put your lifestyle in order – by understanding the limits of your possibilities, so that you do not shoulder tasks that exceed your strengths. Habits provide us with security and help us to organize our daily life. They make life reliable and predictable.

Even if the potential for manipulation in this association is small, it nevertheless exists. There is a danger of getting stuck in the daily chores, wearing yourself out in tackling mundane things and worries and thereby losing sight of the big picture. This can result in ambitious aims and dreams sinking into oblivion. The encounter with the sixth sign involves a certain amount of introspectiveness and coziness – but it is precisely this comfort that can become dangerous for you. These qualities are not only used unknowingly by your counterpart, but are consciously exploited with the intention of committing you – whether in a friendship, an emotional relationship or a working relationship.

Yet another possibility for manipulation is constantly

appealing to your sense of responsibility. This way, you are forced to take responsibility for somebody else's well-being and make bad compromises, which in the long-term will make you unhappy. Although in principle, relationships with persons of the sixth sign are well suited to be particularly long-term and stable in nature as well as lending themselves to solving problems together, it is nevertheless possible for this habit to very quickly result in boredom.

7th topic "partnership": You and persons of your opposite sign

Thereby it is a matter of one of the following connections:

You	Your opponent
Aries	Libra
Taurus	Scorpio
Gemini	Sagittarius
Cancer	Capricorn
Leo	Aquarius
Virgo	Pisces
Libra	Aries
Scorpio	Taurus
Sagittarius	Gemini
Capricorn	Cancer
Aquarius	Leo
Pisces	Virgo

It is necessary to pay particular attention to persons of our seventh sign, as this is the sign that lies directly opposite ours in the zodiac. Persons of your seventh sign are the direct opposite to you, because the seventh sign of the zodiac lies opposite to your sign. In this case, the manipulative capacity of both partners in this association is roughly the same. As these two signs beautifully complement each other in many personal attributes and character traits, they can learn a lot from each other.

If you show a certain degree of understanding and flexibility for each other, such a relationship can be extremely exciting and interesting. However, if this requirement is not met, then the relationship may result in tension or even hostility. In fact, a mutually stimulating rivalry can have a psychologically and emotionally adverse effect on you, and would ultimately lead you into a manipulative trap. The manipulative arsenal of your seventh sign is manifold indeed. In this manner, these persons make great use of charm, compliments and diplomacy on you to achieve their aims.

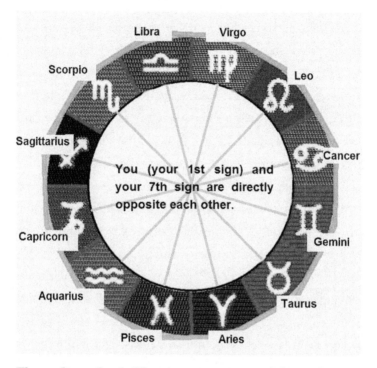

The zodiac wheel. The opposing signs of the zodiac are connected to each other by grey lines

Your colleagues of the seventh sign will clearly and effectively convey to you how to construct your thoughts, intentions and plans so that they gain significant influence on others. The chances are high that you will repeatedly have to resolve various conflicts and disputes with these persons, because circumstances often result in precisely these persons becoming your direct adversaries in the course of your life.

With these persons, it is often a question of partners or enemies. This means that you deal with the personalities of the seventh sign regularly and intensively. And your attention in this regard is well warranted: firstly, you have to investigate and work out the personality of your counterpart (seventh sign) in order to cope with their envy and aggression. Secondly, it often happens that you rely on their help and capabilities. The reason for such direct manipulation between these two diametrically opposed signs is to be found in the fact that each of the 6 axes in the zodiac involves contradictory extremes and polarities. For example, the wild and conflict-seeking Aries pairs up with the cultivated and harmonious Libra, or the family-oriented and sensitive Cancer with the career-focused and cold Capricorn. These examples clearly demonstrate that the manipulative potential of the seventh sign is not insignificant - due to its contrary nature.

The seventh sign teaches us a lesson on the subjects of "appeal", "desire" and "attractiveness". It is difficult for us to ignore persons of the seventh sign: as rivals we either hate or envy them, as friends or partners we feel a strong attraction to them. Sexual desire and a certain eroticism often play a role in the relationship to these persons. Irrespective of the direction, in which such an encounter takes you, it invariably represents a challenge for you and your self-image. You will begin to ask yourself "Am I good enough?" or "Am I desirable?" since the seventh sign casts doubt upon this. This may lead to self-doubt and even the feeling of powerlessness. Rejection and variety can constantly alternate with each other when in contact with persons of the seventh sign, thereby throwing you into confusion. Often, however, these are only transitional phases in an important process, into which persons of the seventh sign can bring you.

Such a challenge in your everyday life can stimulate you to new ambitions and provide you with important impulses on how you can better find your way in the world and obtain what you desire – whether it be in material, professional, partner or spiritual terms. The seventh sign symbolizes the universal power of attraction, which is constantly active and makes our wishes come true – in the true sense of the word. From persons of the seventh sign you learn to attract the things you desire and how to act as a magnet for positive events.

You begin to test and improve your own market value, which will transform your life situation for the better in many areas. Indeed, you can also develop for the better in your private life. Self-love and self-acceptance are the most important prerequisites to enter into a fulfilling partnership. The seventh sign teaches you to accept yourself as well as consider yourself with affection. This positive attitude to yourself will, in turn, have a particularly attractive effect on others.

Nevertheless, the encounter with the seventh sign is also fraught with dangers. For example, the process from self-doubt to self-love may fail, leaving you with your self-awareness damaged. It may be particularly stressful if the encounter with the seventh sign turns into a competitive or even hostile situation. The seventh sign is able to manipulate you by addressing one of the most intensive needs a person knows: the wish to be loved and accepted for his own sake. Persons in this relationship with you will play on this wish and make you do their bidding. A typical sentence would be: "I like you as you are but..." followed by a never-ending stream of allegedly well-intentioned advice. If, on the other hand, a positive relationship is possible with a person of the seventh sign, it will be characterized by deep mutual love and trust. This depends on how much both partners are willing to invest in the relationship.

8th topic "crises and power": You and persons of your eighth sign

This involves one of the following associations:

You	Your opponent
Aries	Scorpio
Taurus	Sagittarius
Gemini	Capricorn
Cancer	Aquarius
Leo	Pisces
Virgo	Aries
Libra	Taurus
Scorpio	Gemini
Sagittarius	Cancer
Capricorn	Leo
Aquarius	Virgo
Pisces	Libra

Always be on your guard when coming into contact with your eighth sign because it has considerable influence on you. Such an alliance features dramatic states of crisis, misfortunes and intensive experiences. Your eighth sign exerts the strongest manipulative force on you. It is not uncommon that you do not immediately sense the powerful aura of such a person on your sign. For this reason, contacts with these persons often prove to be particularly difficult. Every kind of relationship with your eighth sign – whether private, friendly or business – is dangerous because it can result in you suffering a lot of stress and loss in the final outcome.

Even if persons of your eighth sign mean well with you, they may still unintentionally cause harm to you – and if they do it deliberately, they won't have any problem at all! Although you may not infrequently enjoy the most exciting moments of your life together with persons of your eighth sign, it is, of course, also necessary to take account of the other side of the coin and this means confronting the darkest and most horrible moments and crises that it is possible to experience with such an alliance.

Contact with the eighth sign involves drastic experiences in life, major gains and losses, sudden recovery and fatal illness, material rise and fall. Such experiences are an essential element of our life and shape us like few other events can. They call everything into question that we think we know about life and ourselves. Each crisis is simultaneously a challenge for us to understand, to check our convictions and behaviour and – when in doubt – adapt. In this regard, the subject of death can be perceived as an inward death of long-standing personality traits. It is precisely these traits that we are confronted by with the eighth sign. We frequently feel utterly attracted by these persons, even though we already suspect that the risk of getting hurt is extremely high. For it is never boring with these persons, even though a lasting relationship with them can prove very demanding.

A paradox thus arises: when you are together – you feel constrained, when you are alone – you get bored. Extremely intensive experiences are collected in this union, which provide not only dazzling excitement and inspiration but also dramatic disappointments and hatred. In time, such a restless union will lead to a dead-end and your eighth sign will lose interest in you.

The lesson to be learned from persons of the eighth sign is how to fail properly. Crises affect everybody – the crucial factor is how to deal with them. Although our eighth sign teaches us where our weaknesses and strengths lie, it does it in a painful way. Persons of our eighth sign have the ability to recognise your weaknesses relatively quickly, which also gives them a lot of influence and power over you. You run great risks in arguments and confrontations with your eighth sign, while the chances of a favourable outcome for you are extremely low.

Business undertakings with these persons as partners are like a roller-coaster ride – you can win a lot but also lose a lot. Contacts with your eighth sign exert contrasting and alternating effects on you. For example, they can assume a transformational, regenerative or destructive nature – depending on the circumstances.

It is hardly possible for you to encounter a person of the eighth sign without being influenced or even manipulated by them in one way or another. The best way of handling this is to be aware of these circumstances. Fear is the wrong reaction – you should regard the encounter rather as a possibility of learning something about the most difficult and final things both in life and yourself. It takes courage to face up to your own weaknesses. Persons of the eighth sign have a sure knack of putting their finger on our weak spots and thus challenging us to develop ourselves.

9th topic "meaningfulness": You and persons of your ninth sign

Thereby it is a matter of one of the following connections:

You	Your opponent
Aries	Sagittarius
Taurus	Capricorn
Gemini	Aquarius
Cancer	Pisces
Leo	Aries
Virgo	Taurus
Libra	Gemini
Scorpio	Cancer
Sagittarius	Leo
Capricorn	Virgo
Aquarius	Libra
Pisces	Scorpio

We continue our path through the constellations of the zodiac. Following the bleak challenges involved in encountering persons of the eighth sign, we now meet persons of the ninth sign, with whom we develop relationships full of ease and harmony.

In contact with your ninth sign, you do not generally have any major manipulative experiences – quite the contrary, in fact, as you usually get on well with these persons: the intensive discussions you have absolutely inspire you. You grapple with the philosophical issues of faith, religion and the meaning of life and adjust your life accordingly. In this manner, you can train your abstract thinking in contexts while experiencing further positive influences on your awareness. Concentrating on these areas of life is crucial for a happy and full life in the holistic sense. The ninth sign provides the nutrition to your spirit and soul that you crave and which is all too readily neglected in daily life. We now primarily enter into spiritual contact with our environment; in the relationship with the ninth sign, material values play little to no role at all.

Manipulative influences of the ninth sign are revealed by these persons attempting to missionise you and make use of sermons to impose their philosophies and views upon you. In these partnerships, you can sometimes be seduced into all kinds of trips or even into moving home. Extremely beneficial to you is the tendency of your ninth sign to expand your horizon, teach you new knowledge and stimulate your spiritual growth. Such a person can be very advantageous to you in business dealings by advising and teaching you. Such a union is generally quite harmonious for all kinds of associations, whether they be business relations, in marriage, in friendship, etc.

First and foremost, your ninth sign helps you in the search for meaning in life. Whether these entire philosophies and enhancement of knowledge, with which these people provide you, will guide you in a direction desired is something you should regularly think about with a critical mind. For these contacts also contain negative aspects – namely that you might adopt false ideologies and a distorted perception and be taken in by charlatans. Your character is subjected to a severe test, since contact with new philosophies and knowledge invariably harbours a risk of becoming arrogant or fanatical. Your ninth sign tends to communicate with you in abstract concepts that may confuse you. This is in contrast to your third sign, who generally speaks to you in clear and concrete terms. Sometimes, expansive tendencies emanate from your ninth sign that consist of these persons attempting to acquire more power and influence over you.

Contacts with these persons will help you to gain a wide range of thoughts concerning the events and experiences you encounter. What you should embrace in this regard is the ability to both analyse your accumulated experiences and draw conclusions as to their usefulness.

Contact with persons of your ninth sign is a great enrichment if it involves spiritual realignment and further development. If you should find yourself at such a point in your life, then this encounter holds a lot of good things in store for you. Take care, however, not to lose your equilibrium while also dedicating sufficient attention to the other aspects of your life.

10th topic "pursuit of success": You and persons of your tenth sign

This involves one of the following associations:

You	Your opponent
Aries	Capricorn
Taurus	Aquarius
Gemini	Pisces
Cancer	Aries
Leo	Taurus
Virgo	Gemini
Libra	Cancer
Scorpio	Leo
Sagittarius	Virgo
Capricorn	Libra
Aquarius	Scorpio
Pisces	Sagittarius

Let us now consider the tenth sign in the zodiac. The relationship to persons of your tenth sign is of a completely different nature to those of your ninth sign. We commonly encounter the tenth sign in the person of the superior, the leader or – in general terms – the person who attempts to force his will upon us and dominate us. It is easy to recognise that although such an association also possesses a high manipulative potential, it also contains the opportunity for professional and social advancement for us. Our tenth sign challenges us in the areas of industriousness, ambition, career and self-discipline and will invariably give you the feeling of being vastly superior to you.

The manipulative capability of your tenth sign is expressed by these persons frequently playing the role of a boss for you. This means that the tenth sign is always trying to order you around and make you dance to his tune. For this reason, this kind of manipulation is not at all difficult to see through. Nevertheless, such an alliance may work well, provided that both partners respond to each other with sufficient understanding. Otherwise, this can cause an extremely tense relationship for both partners. If you get on well with such a partner, then both of you can enjoy successes together in business, because this is an excellent alliance in this regard. Despite the tendency of your tenth sign always wanting to keep a firm hold on the reins, these persons not uncommonly provide you with possibilities of improving your place in society. It happens that these persons readily note and recognise your performance and endeavours. They notice your successes more strongly than those of others.

Be aware that the tenth sign invariably attempts to impose obligations and responsibilities on you. And this mostly happens in a clear and direct manner. In order to prevent undesirable commands from these persons, you should develop your own principles and opinions, which, in turn, will lead to favourable decisions for you – decisions you will then strongly defend. From time to time, your tenth sign may act arrogantly and unfairly towards you. Prevent such tendencies.

It would prove beneficial for you have the opportunity to learn and adopt those methods from your tenth sign, which you then use yourself to improve your performance and discipline. Even if these persons appear lazy and ineffective, you can still benefit from them if you pay closer attention. For your tenth sign reveals precisely these secrets in a quite natural way, because it projects the principle of the Tenth House onto you. The ability to make everyday decisions quickly and sensibly on a regular basis is extremely important. In this regard, your tenth sign can enhance your progress by helping you to develop this ability.

11th topic "friendship": You and persons of your eleventh sign

Thereby it is a matter of one of the following connections:

You	Your opponent
Aries	Aquarius
Taurus	Pisces
Gemini	Aries
Cancer	Taurus
Leo	Gemini
Virgo	Cancer
Libra	Leo
Scorpio	Virgo
Sagittarius	Libra
Capricorn	Scorpio
Aquarius	Sagittarius
Pisces	Capricorn

We now come to the penultimate sign in the constellations of the zodiac. An intensive and long-lasting friendship is associated with persons of your eleventh sign. Many good friends of yours are probably from this sign. This is perhaps the reason why you show a lot of respect for these persons. This is exactly where the manipulative potential of your eleventh sign lies. These persons often attempt to give the appearance of virtually assuming the role of your patron and protégé. Often, however, they just do it as if they were favourable and beneficial for you.

Although hopes and desires play a major role in your relationship with these persons, themes such as freedom and shaping a better world are also involved. Persons of your eleventh sign know how to represent themselves as something special. They are frequently trend-setters and are very sociable. This may lead to a condescending attitude towards everybody else – particularly you. In order to soak up the admiration of others, they convey a false appearance. Beware of possible hypocrisies.

Persons of your eleventh sign will give you incentives to think individually and freely and cause you to rethink your original values and views on various themes. As you frequently engage with persons of your eleventh sign with regard to similar interests, these persons attach great hope to you and thus provide you with support. Sometimes, patrons are encountered among your eleventh sign, who are prepared to fund your ideas. You can also realise social projects and visions with persons of your eleventh sign, as you can mostly rely on them.

It is, however, necessary to distinguish between real and false friends, since your eleventh sign can also provide you with false friends who then attempt to lull you with praise and comfort while pursuing their own goals. When persons of your eleventh sign are too egocentric and self-assured, their positive aspects are transformed into negative ones. It is up to you to recognise this tendency and distance yourself from it. Do not allow yourself to become harnessed to goals dictated to by others!

Generally, however, positive aspects dominate in the relationship with the eleventh sign. These persons can introduce you into new social circles and clubs, which, in turn, will raise your standing in the social world. Here it is also probable that persons of your eleventh sign are able to predict several future events that will take place in your life. This is because the eleventh sign is also tuned to you from a precognitive perspective – due to the fact you yourself are the third sign for your eleventh sign. The longer you have a close relationship with a person of your eleventh sign, the more likely it will be that that person will tell you some of these predictions. These prophecies, however, are not usually particularly important, not always correct and have to be taken with a grain of salt. Your eleventh sign may also establish contacts for you to good business partners, with whom you will get on with very well – this, in turn, leading to you all being able to effectively represent your common interests together.

12th topic "secrets": You and persons of your twelfth sign

This involves one of the following associations:

You	Your opponent
Aries	Pisces
Taurus	Aries
Gemini	Taurus
Cancer	Gemini
Leo	Cancer
Virgo	Leo
Libra	Virgo
Scorpio	Libra
Sagittarius	Scorpio
Capricorn	Sagittarius
Aquarius	Capricorn
Pisces	Aquarius

We have now reached the end of the constellations of the zodiac – at your twelfth sign. Every kind of relationship with your twelfth sign is characterised by difficulties and confusions. These are encounters that are elusive of understanding and are enveloped by an air of mystery and secrecy. These often problematic alliances involve your secret enemies or persons who have a great potential to become vicious and hostile in the course of time. Persons of your twelfth sign often gain your trust for the purpose of delving into your hidden secrets. And they are usually very successful in this. If it suits their purposes, they can reveal your secrets in public and so discredit you or simply harm you – for whatever reason they may have in doing so. This is the great manipulative risk involved with your twelfth sign. You should always be on your guard against these persons, particularly if you are associated with them in business relationships. Be aware that the persons normally know more about you than you would like them to. Relationships and friendships with your twelfth sign usually get off to a good start. However, there is a strong likelihood that in the course of time you will be cheated or betrayed. In the worst case, this may result in these persons bringing about your death.

Another important manipulative characteristic of your twelfth sign is expressed in the fact that these persons invariably attempt to control you in a covert manner. Yes, you may not even notice, but the control and guidance emanates from your twelfth sign and it does everything at its own discretion. If no discord or disagreements should occur in a private relationship, the twelfth sign is able to exercise forebearance in relation to your weaknesses and suppress its secret hostility towards you.

Persons of your twelfth sign possess the potential to charm you and cloud your mind. The manipulations emanating from this sign are actually the most difficult to detect, as they very often occur in secret. You lack insight into these persons, and they can exercise a sedative effect on you. It is possible for your perception to become distorted or even partly to dissolve when in the presence of these persons. Persons of the twelfth sign can appear mysterious and secretive to you.

If you come into conflict with persons of your twelfth sign, then you are in trouble. Waging open war on these persons would – in any case – be fruitless. This is because everything such a person undertakes against you is not directly detectable, but only via traces and symptoms, which hint at malicious intrigues and intentions. The only way you can proceed against your secretly acting enemies is to uncover and reveal their deeds. Unmask your enemies, since this way they will lose their strengths and be dissolved in the glare of the sun's rays like vampires in direct sunlight.

The spiritual incentives unleashed by a prolonged contact with your twelfth sign are to be found in the realisation that there is a difference between sensible goals and deceptive illusions. If you chase illusions, it means that you intend to distance yourself from the real world. And allowing yourself to become intoxicated by your own dream worlds and visions bearing no relation to reality is often a path leading into the abyss. Such behaviour in fact results in self-destruction. The reasons for this are often to be found in escapism: this way, reality can be perceived as pain, resulting in the strong intensity of your feelings becoming unbearable.

II. The manipulative abilities of the various signs of the zodiac

In the first part, we have observed how the individual signs of the zodiac influence you according to your relationship to them in the zodiac. In this part, we intend to consider how the individual signs of the zodiac behave in relation to the other signs and manipulate them.

Each sign we encounter basically symbolises either traits that we carry within ourselves or stages of life we pass through. This aspect is also symbolised in astrology by the various Houses, each of which is characterised by a sign of the zodiac. These mechanisms arise from the universal Law of Correspondence, also known as the Principle of Analogy. This means that everything is interlinked and so has an equivalent at every level. "As in great so in small, as within so without, as above so below." Everything we perceive externally is a mirror of our inner nature. Each person combines aspects of others in himself in varying degrees. The aspects embodied in the signs of the zodiac and their Houses are a part of our personality, our path in life and our environment. Those who understand the relations and systematologies find it easy to recognise the various aspects in others and benefit from them.

The manipulative abilities of the various signs of the zodiac

Not every sign of the zodiac possesses a force of equal power to manipulate another sign. It depends both on the sign of your counterpart and the theme, under which they meet, how strongly they make an impact. The influence exerted is always in both directions. This means that every contact with another person possesses the potential to both influence and manipulate us.

However, if you embrace the Cosmic Laws, which are expressed in the symbols of the signs of the zodiac and their Houses, you will find it much easier to distance yourself from undesirable influences, thereby protecting yourself while simultaneously being able to increase your manipulative power on others. The following text is intended to demonstrate how and under what auspices the individual signs of the zodiac exert their manipulation, at which vulnerable points or character traits they start and how it is possible to identify this kind of manipulation. You will undoubtedly be familiar with many of the examples of manipulation described here, albeit without having been hitherto aware that this manipulation ensues on the basis of the signs of the zodiac.

Our sign shapes our character and our destiny, while also determining how we react to persons of other signs. Even before we are ever conscious of ourselves following our birth, the power of the signs of the zodiac influence us and set the course for our life. This is the reason why the potential for manipulation based on our star sign is so great and thereby commonly underestimated. The following pages provide an instrument designed for you to better understand not only your own reactions, but – first and foremost – the influence of others on you and your decisions as well as identify possible manipulations.

1. How the Aries manipulates

The signs of the zodiac begin with Aries. This is one of the spring zodiacal signs. Persons born under the sign of Aries are characterised as being determined and purposeful in putting their ideas into practice. They are very good both at expressing themselves and at self-realisation. Their strong features are strength of personality and character. They bubble with a zest for action. Patience, restraint and tactfulness are not included in their strong points, but instead a healthy egoism and the ability to assert themselves in the world. Aries are honest and loyal; hypocrisy and guile are foreign to them. They are persons of action – not of long periods of reflection. As the representative of the 1st House, this star sign stands for our encounter with the world and the recognition of the individual "I" in distinction to the collective "you".

Aries and Aries

The two of them are the first sign for each other in each case. Their relationship is characterised by a high degree of understanding and familiarity. An Aries can manipulate another Aries by giving him the feeling that he is completely infallible and is always right in his opinions – behaviour that inevitably leads to conflicts with his environment. An Aries knows that another Aries loves to be the centre of attention and is keen on charging ahead. He can use this knowledge to his own benefit and incite him to such behaviour.

Aries and Taurus

Here a particularly intensive effect is revealed. For the Taurus, the Aries is the 12th sign – he thus embodies a sense of mystery and being clouded in secrecy. The Aries is invariably a step ahead of the Taurus. He knows the weaknesses of the Taurus – approaching life in a rather leisurely manner and being addicted to physical and material pleasures, while the Taurus admires the Aries for his courage and strength of personality. The Aries manipulates the Taurus by seducing him into activities, the consequences of which the Taurus is unable to measure. This may include drugs or risky business dealings – and also sexual seduction. From the perspective of the Taurus, something secretive and thus fascinating is inherent in everything. Quite deliberately, the Aries exploits the weaknesses of the Taurus for easy money, a comfortable way of life and all kinds of pleasures. The Taurus needs a secure environment and reliable relationships. The Aries seduces him into abandoning them and undergoing risks that can well be to the disadvantage of the Taurus. As the Taurus's 12th sign, the Aries symbolises the potential loss of self at all levels.

Aries and Gemini

For the Gemini, the Aries is the eleventh sign. Although Geminis have a wide range of interests and often possess a large number of talents, a Gemini lacks the single-mindedness of an Aries. It is very easy for his inner compass to fall out of balance and for him to lose himself in his interests. As the Gemini's eleventh sign, the Aries encounters him as a friend, this resulting in the successful combination of their extremely different dispositions. From the Aries, the Gemini learns to concentrate on his goals without becoming distracted. Nevertheless, the risk exists that the Aries will cause the Gemini to pursue interests that are not really his own but only benefit the Aries. Particularly since the Gemini often does not know what he wants, the clear line and goals of the Aries appear all too appealing to him – even though in the beginning he is not clear whether these goals are really his own. The Aries can talk the Gemini into believing that he is not good or strong enough or indeed not able to live properly and therefore permanently dependent on the advice of others. By this means, the Gemini gains the impression of not being able to make decisions himself. The Aries sells him this under the premise that it is "all for his own good."

Aries and Cancer

For the Cancer, the Aries is the tenth sign. He encounters the sensitive and artistically talented Cancer at the level of the pursuit of success and this may have fatal consequences for the Cancer. The Cancer is fond of withdrawing into himself and can be emotionally hurt. He needs creative freedom in order to flourish. The Cancer has little resistance to offer against the strong personality of the Aries, who confronts him in the person of a superior, leader or other figure of authority, and can all too easily be dominated. As the Aries lacks understanding for the needs of the Cancer, he denies the Cancer the creative freedom of development, thus making him unhappy and depressed in the long-term. Rather than subtle manipulation, here we encounter the clearly recognisable dominance of the Aries over the Cancer, which the Cancer is only able to evade by withdrawal and distance.

The manipulative abilities of the various signs of the zodiac

Aries and Leo

The Aries encounters the Leo as his ninth sign. The Leo, as befitting a fire sign, virtually radiates energy and zest for action, and for this reason is a worthy opponent to the Aries. The manipulative potential of the Aries on the Leo is limited – instead it commonly manifests itself in a positive, reciprocal influence, in which the Leo experiences the Aries as a spiritual advisor who can help him keep his temperament under control. A latent tendency exists for the Aries to attempt to enthuse the Leo for ideological matters, but here the Leo does not allow himself to fooled by such spiritual restrictions for very long.

Aries and Virgo

For the Virgo, the Aries is the eighth sign. Virgos are characterised by their strong sense of order. How they think and act is rooted in reality, and they are not prone to daydreaming. This is why Virgos usually come through crises relatively unscathed. It is different, though, if they are manipulated by an Aries. The Aries succeeds in shaking the Virgo's sense of reality and bringing chaos and disorder into his life. The Aries constantly attempts to persuade the Virgo that his perception is false and the way he deals with problems is not the right one. This denudes the Virgo of his self-confidence, intimidates him and triggers endless self-criticism. This results in the risk of his psyche being destroyed. Virgos frequently feel attracted to Aries (a fire sign) and admire their resolve and determination. This is why they therefore take the Aries' criticism to heart and cast doubt upon themselves.

Aries and Libra

For the Libra, the Aries is the seventh sign. A strong attraction exists between Aries and Libra, which not uncommonly results in productive partnerships both in the private and business sphere. Libras loves beauty and aestheticism and has many good ideas that can prove successful, when combined with the determination of an Aries. However, it is not unusual for the Aries to envy the Libra for his inventiveness, and this may result in rivalries. The Aries can use the Libra's ideas as his own and go behind the Libra's back. Notwithstanding this, the Libra finds it difficult to avoid the attraction that the Aries as the seventh sign exerts on him, so that this can lead to a strong love-hate relationship. The Aries manipulates the Libra by pretending

to be his ally and partner, while all the time hatching other
plans in the background.

Aries and Scorpio

For the Scorpio, the Aries is the sixth sign. This association
is particularly complex, since although the encounter with
the sixth sign stands under the heading "compromise", while
the passionate Scorpio is known for not entering into
compromises as well as being very belligerent. Nevertheless,
the perseverance and tenacity of the Aries can still make him
accept compromises in some cases. This can have a positive
effect on the life of the Scorpio and act as a stabilising factor.
At the same time, however, there is a risk of frustration and
dissatisfaction mounting in the Scorpio to the extent that he
feels a virtual prisoner. This dissatisfaction can be discharged
in the form of arguments and even violence. The Aries
manipulates the Scorpio by forcing him into many
compromises against his nature and emotionally
blackmailing him. A Scorpio will, admittedly, rarely be happy
in these circumstances.

Aries and Sagittarius

The Aries is the fifth sign for the Sagittarius. The relationship between these two signs is primarily characterised by creativity, albeit only being a secondary factor for the Sagittarius. The Sagittarius is a thoroughly moral person, for whom a sense of honour, pride and reputation are extremely important. He tends to regard creative outbursts with suspicion. The Aries can induce him to cast aside this mistrust – at least for a while – and enter uncharted waters, this bringing new impulses into the Sagittarius' life. The risk of manipulation ensuing in this association is based on the danger that the Sagittarius will weaken his moral principles and will change under the influence of the Aries. The Aries achieves this by reproaching the Sagittarius that his convictions are false or by specifically damaging his reputation by spreading rumours.

Aries and Capricorn

For the Capricorn, the Aries is the fourth sign. Capricorns are characterised by their great ambition and pragmatism. They attach great value to diligence and discipline and unswervingly pursue their goals. In doing so, they risk missing out on the good and lighter sides of life. This aspect is intensified by contact with the Aries. The Aries makes the

Capricorn believe that he can only attain his goals by pursuing them along familiar paths. This way, he severely restricts the Capricorn's potential for success. The Capricorn is receptive to appeals to his awareness for tradition, and it is precisely this point that the Aries aims at. There are similarities between these two signs – both are of a determined nature and both possess a strong drive. However, while the Capricorn is more of a cool analyst, the Aries is – in contrast – an impulsive firebrand. He is able to give the Capricorn advice, not act in such an undercooled way and look after his own family.

Aries and Aquarius

For the Aquarius, the Aries is the third sign. The two signs are often associated with a humorous and intensive friendship. They have fun together and celebrate their friendship in a grandiose manner. They mutually inspire and encourage each other. However, the Aries rarely tolerates sharing his place at the centre of attention with the Aquarius. For this reason, as his third sign he manipulates him by availing himself of hypocritical statements and rumours in order to damage the Aquarius' popularity and image. Aquariuses attach great value to friendships – indeed they are simply unable to exist without them. This is where the Aries' manipulation gets to work, by isolating the Aquarius through insinuation and spreading rumours, thus depriving him of his most important resources. As a result, the Aries is able to sun himself in the attraction of the Aquarius without having to fear that the other is superior to him.

Aries and Pisces

For the Pisces, the Aries is the second sign. Pisces are generally very sensitive and compassionate in their nature. Because of their vulnerability, they often withdraw from the world in order to protect themselves. Although, as his second sign, the Aries embodies exactly the opposite with his dare-devil manner, Aries' manipulative power on the Pisces is quite insignificant. The Aries will attempt to fully win over the Pisces in order to tie them to him, but as he will never succeed in completely understanding the nature of the Pisces and their needs, such an attachment will rarely be of long duration.

2. How the Taurus manipulates

Persons born under the sign of Taurus are generally extremely pragmatic and down-to-earth, and do not readily lose their composure. Their virtues do not include an exaggerated ambition – but they are able to enjoy life in all its aspects. What motivates them are aspects such as material possessions, image and reputation, social and financial security as well as the creation of a secure basis of life. These aspects also characterise the 2nd House, which Taurus precedes. Tauruses are characterised by their good disposition. Although not prone to quick reactions, once they have decided to act, then their reactions are vehement and irrevocable. Their strong points are endurance and resilience, although they are all too easily seduced by pleasure and cosiness.

Taurus and Taurus

Taurus and Taurus encounter each other as the first sign. Their relationship is characterised by understanding and fundamental agreement. As partners and friends, their thoughtful actions can provide a sense of reality to projects and decisions while putting a break on the hot-headed ideas or daydreams of other signs. A Taurus manipulates another

Taurus by making it all too cosy for him in his comfort zone – this resulting in the Taurus neglecting his goals and ambitions without being aware of it. Sometimes it is necessary in life to strive for something in order to achieve something – even if this entails risks or expending great effort.

Taurus and Gemini

For the Gemini, the Taurus is the twelfth sign. In the positive sense, the Taurus can help the Gemini to acquire a more down-to-earth attitude. On the negative side, however, the Taurus can also have a literally paralysing effect on the Gemini. The Gemini begins to neglect his own wide-ranging interests and virtually comes to a standstill. The Taurus achieves this by capturing the Gemini's attention with practical and material questions of life and giving him the impression that it is these questions that constitute the content and meaning of life. The Gemini needs new ideas and spiritual development as much as the air he breathes. He is constantly in search of new intellectual challenges. The Taurus is able to seduce him into pleasure, apathy and idleness, with the result that the Gemini neglects his talents.

Taurus and Cancer

For the Cancer, the Taurus is the eleventh sign. As their relationship stands under the heading "friendship", it is therefore often positive. Taurus and Cancer complement each other, since the Cancer is more creative while the Taurus is more down-to-earth. If a Taurus wishes to manipulate a Cancer, then he achieves it by making the Cancer unsure of his effect on others. He talks him into being more suspicious of other people and observe their signals and utterances more critically. This can lead to the Cancer turning inwards more than usual and ultimately becoming lonely.

Taurus and Leo

For the Leo, the Taurus is the tenth sign. The Taurus frequently behaves as the Leo's superior or supervisor, which is difficult to reconcile with his huge ego. The Taurus envies the Leo for his impact in public and his popularity – and this is where he works at manipulating him. The Taurus knows that the Leo is susceptible to flattery and insults and makes use of both of these for his manipulating. Sometimes he will praise him to the skies only to dress him down in public in front of others and give his judgement the legitimacy of absolute authority and objectivity, thus making any objection pointless. The actual arbitrariness of this action will unnerve the Leo and cause him to doubt his own abilities.

Taurus and Virgo

For the Virgo, the Taurus is the ninth sign. In principle, the two signs complement each other extremely well, even though the Taurus can be too untidy for the Virgo's liking. The Taurus can entice the Virgo into taking a more relaxed view and devoting himself to pleasures and an easy life. The danger here is that the Virgo absolutely needs this orderliness and organisation to feel good. If the Taurus uses distractions to prevent this from happening, there is a risk for the Virgo either that he either loses touch with himself or serious conflicts occur. If the Taurus wishes to manipulate the Virgo, he will surprise him with spontaneous trips and appointments and disturb Virgo's normal routine with professions of sympathy and gifts that seem positive at first sight.

Taurus and Libra

For the Libra, the Taurus is the eighth sign. Libras are not good at handling crises. The Taurus can help them to improve this ability while accepting that failure is also part of life. In crisis situations, the Taurus can provide eminently practical tips, which have an immediate effect. The manipulative potential of this relationship lies in a possible dependence of the Libra on the Taurus, the Libra henceforth taking the Taurus' suggestions as laws to base a successful and content life on, a view that the Taurus is only too keen on confirming by appropriate utterances.

Taurus and Scorpio

As is the case with all seventh signs, a strong attraction exists between Taurus and Scorpio. The Taurus finds it easy to seduce the Scorpio – including sexually – by specifically awakening and feeding his passions. Although the Taurus' capability for pleasure and the Scorpio's passion can lead to fireworks of desire and devotion, these relationships are rarely of long duration. The Scorpio does not like the fact that it so difficult to ruffle the Taurus – he seeks fights and confrontations, heated discussions and a gain in knowledge. This, though, is not possible with the Taurus. It is easy for the Scorpio to manipulate the Taurus by making him jealous in a precisely targeted manner, thus bringing him out of his shell.

Taurus and Sagittarius

For the Sagittarius, the Taurus is the sixth sign. When it is a question of moral convictions, the Sagittarius is only rarely prepared to undertake pragmatic compromises. However, this is precisely what the Taurus compels him to do. He requests the Sagittarius not to perceive things in an overly narrow manner – which can be very beneficial for the Sagittarius. The latter's sense of identity, however, is based on defending these moral principles as well as his pride. In the event that he softens his attitude, then this can result in an identity crisis with an unknown outcome since his reputation will suffer as a consequence. The others admire him for his moral integrity and intransigence. It is possible for the relativisation of these characteristics to convulse his entire social environment and reveal the Sagittarius as a hypocrite.

Taurus and Capricorn

This encounter involves two signs with horns on their heads, neither of whom are fundamentally prepared to compromise on their own determination. For this reason, a lively partnership and friendship can result from this association which flourishes on the basis of mutual support and pragmatism. If the Taurus wishes to manipulate the Capricorn, then he eggs him on to ever greater ambition until he overestimates his powers, falters and tumbles, while the Taurus casually leans back and watches.

Taurus and Aquarius

For the Aquarius, the Taurus is the fourth sign. Although the Aquarius has basically little in common with the subject of tradition that dominates this relationship, this is exactly where the Taurus gets to work. He talks the Aquarius into dealing with things more in a traditional way and not to allow himself to be guided by his unconventional desires and ideas. He reminds him that this is the reason for his previous failures. However, the Aquarius is a free spirit, for whom conservative values are poison.

Taurus and Pisces

For the Pisces, the Taurus is the third sign. If the Taurus attempts to manipulate the Pisces, then he will represent him as unreliable and dreamy to others, thus making them change their attitude to the Pisces. By comments of this type, he will unsettle the Pisces and give him the feeling of being unable to live his daily life alone and therefore needing constant guidance and instruction.

Taurus and Aries

For the Aries, the Taurus is the second sign. In this relationship, the Taurus only possesses a small amount of manipulative potential. Instead, it is often the case that he helps the Aries to discover his talents and abilities. The Aries will admire the Taurus for his strength and poise and thereby fall into self-doubt himself. Tauruses give Aries the impression that they frequently snub others and are not welcome as a result. This can lead either to withdrawal and isolation on the part of the Aries, or to making his behaviour to others even more non-committal than is already the case. This will cost him many important friends.

3. How the Gemini manipulates

Geminis are multifaceted personalities who frequently attract attention by their strong intellect or other talents. They possess complex personalities and are often even contradictory – the have, as the saying goes, two faces. They symbolise the puberty stage of life, which involves spiritual growth, exploration and criticism, learning and communication. "Who do I want to be?" is one of the typical questions that the Gemini asks himself. Although the Gemini possesses an agile mind, pondering about things for a long time and concentration are not part of his repertoire. They find it easy to look at the bigger picture although often being buffeted by rapidly changing emotional states of mind and only rarely reveal themselves as predictable and stable. For this reason, their potential manipulation is especially high. The Third House, which they precede, is characterised by communication with the environment. This is why Geminis often make good mediators.

Gemini and Gemini

Geminis often have the feeling that nobody in the world understands them. They feel out of place and lonely. Another Gemini, however, understands this feeling and its cause, so that Geminis support each other. Nevertheless, one Gemini can very easily manipulate another Gemini into a cocoon-like life, thus no longer giving other persons the chance to understand him. If one Gemini wishes to manipulate another, then he will talk him into believing that nobody understands him as well as he does, and that he should therefore cut off all other contacts.

Gemini and Cancer

For Cancers, the Gemini is the twelfth sign. Cancers, by their very nature, are receptive to everything mysterious – to that which is not revealed at first sight. It is therefore no surprise that they are utterly fascinated by Geminis and their diversity. This is precisely where the danger lies. This fascination can turn into dependency and addictive behaviour, which the Gemini strengthens by means of contradictory signals. For example, one day he will inform the Cancer that he is very fond of him and appreciates him, only the next day to treat him in a dismissive and detached way. This way, he plunges the Cancer into a deep emotional dependence, in which he believes he is unable to live without the Gemini.

The manipulative abilities of the various signs of the zodiac

Gemini and Leo

An unusual friendship is often associated with Gemini and Leo. The Leo is loud and temperamental, while the Gemini is thoughtful and difficult to understand. For this reason, they rarely compete with each other and are thus able to enjoy the benefits of the other. The Gemini only rarely succeeds in manipulating the Leo, except when he challenges him in an intellectual field and gives the Leo the feeling that he bows to the Leo's superior knowledge. Although the Leo is unable to resist such a challenge, he fails against the Gemini, and this failure hurts his pride.

Gemini and Virgo

For the Virgo, the Gemini is the tenth sign. For the Virgo, success is not as important as maintaining the ordered way of life he is used to. However, in order to impress the Gemini, he can deviate from this. While the Gemini can motivate the Virgo to realise himself and attain new goals, he can also drive the Virgo crazy with his unpredictability. The Virgo is obliged to know where he stands – and it is precisely this certainty that is denied to him by the Gemini. He is at a loss to understand what the Gemini (who commonly appears as his boss or in a superior position) expects from him, and this leads to frustration and self-doubt.

Gemini and Libra

For the Libra, the Gemini is the ninth sign. Here the subject is "broadening of horizons". The Libra is infatuated by the diverse interests of the Gemini and is only all too happy to be inspired by him and beguiled into intellectual flights of fancy. Even so, fairness and balance are important factors for the Libra, and in this regard the Gemini has severe deficits. If a Gemini wishes to manipulate a Libra, then he inveigles him into becoming his accomplice in unfair and arbitrary processes.

Gemini and Scorpio

For the Scorpio, the Gemini is the eighth sign. The passion and belligerence of the Scorpio makes him virtually predestined for conflicts and crises, which the Gemini is skilled in intensifying. He will spur the Scorpio on to plunge into hopeless struggles and reject other persons, so that he will end up all alone in emergencies. Although Geminis possess an agile mind, energy and vigour are not among their strong points. They prefer to stay in the safer waters of intellectual and spiritual ideas – i.e. words and not deeds. They can misuse the Scorpio, assume responsibility for them by suggesting to him it is a matter of struggling for truth, of life and death, there is something so crucial at stake here that under no circumstances can it be given up.

Gemini and Sagittarius

As contradictory as these two star signs might appear at first sight, their relationship is shaped by the aspect of "partnership" and it often possible for their association to result in a successful business model and long-standing friendship, the success of which is based on them giving each other sufficient freedom. The potential for manipulation by the Gemini on the Sagittarius is based on his talking the Sagittarius into deals and businesses that he really does not want.

Gemini and Capricorn

Geminis and Capricorns do not get on with each other very well. Although the Capricorn has no interest in the moods of the Gemini, the fact that that Gemini is his sixth sign leaves him with no other choice than to repeatedly having to listen to the Gemini's criticism. This can demand quite a bit from the Capricorn and even make him unhappy. Emotional arbitrariness is something that he cannot understand and thus becomes an unknown factor in his plans. By this means, the Gemini can drain the Capricorn of energy and – by repeated use of emotional dramas and changes of mood – distract him from achieving his goals.

Gemini and Aquarius

This is an encounter involving two congenial soul-mates. The relationship between an Aquarius and a Gemini is often characterised by a deep understanding and harmony, because the Aquarius is prepared to accept the Gemini as he is. For this reason, his potential for manipulation on the Gemini is stronger than the other way round. As his fifth sign, the Gemini can manipulate the Aquarius by issuing the Aquarius' ideas and plans as his own. As competitive thinking and envy are rather alien concepts for the Aquarius, it will not be an easy matter for him to identify this behaviour and defend himself against it.

Gemini and Pisces

Pisces think and act on gut instinct. They are only rarely able to rationally justify their decisions. The Gemini succeeds in influencing these emotional decisions in accordance with his own wishes by persuading the Pisces that his gut instinct is not consistent with traditional values. In doing so, he benefits from what he can find out about the fundamental intellectual attitudes of the Pisces, and exploits this knowledge against the Pisces in a targeted manner.

Gemini and Aries

The Aries are an easy prey for Geminis. They are aware of the Aries' stubbornness and rather irascible character and accordingly influence him by using clever methods of communication. For example, a Gemini will always suggest the opposite of what he really wants to an Aries, because he knows that the Aries will contradict him and ultimately do the opposite – i.e. precisely what the Gemini wants him to do.

Gemini and Taurus

Taurus, as an earth sign, has by nature a close association to everything material. This is both one of his strong points and part of his weakness that the Gemini knows how to take advantage of. He makes the Taurus worry about the possibility of losing his possessions, thus making him susceptible to manipulations. As the Taurus finds it difficult to follow the Gemini's intellectual flights of fancy, it is a simply matter for the Gemini to persuade the Taurus that he is stupid.

4. How the Cancer manipulates

Cancers are intrinsically very sensitive, which is why they often withdraw from the world. They take emotional injuries and insults to heart. At the same time they are very sensitive and are rather shy in encounters with others. Their sensitivity is also their best instrument of manipulation, because no sign succeeds so well in putting themselves in others' shoes, as does the Cancer. They are soft and act based on their emotions. As a sign of the fourth house, Cancers stand for everything that has to do with our origins, our roots and our heritage. We associate deep-seated feelings with these aspects, which can rarely be influenced by conscious decisions.

Cancer and Cancer

As always with the first sign, mutual understanding and a great accord characterize this relationship. Cancers may, however, bring the other person to completely turn away from the world and others for fear of injury, thereby causing them to miss many beautiful encounters with others.

Cancer and Leo

For the Leo, Cancer is the 12th sign. The Leo admires the empathy of the Cancer, who perceives many nuances that escape Leos in theirs self-centeredness. Therefore, it is easy for the Cancer to manipulate the Leo. Cancers can convince Leos that they does not perceive particular nuances and that others who are superficially friendly are in reality laughing at the Leo. The Leo, however, needs recognition by others as much as the air we breathe. He will believe in such a manipulation without questioning and will be very unhappy about it.

Cancer and Virgo

For the Virgo, Cancer is the eleventh sign. In principle, the two meet in a friendly manner and Virgos benefit from the fact that Cancers are sensitive enough to respond to their needs. The manipulative effect of Cancer on the Virgo is correspondingly low. The Cancer can have a manipulative influence on the Virgo by always appealing to the Virgo's emotional side. To cope with his everyday life, it is often necessary to push personal feelings and problems aside. This works very well for the Virgin. However, Cancers can make appropriate comments that allow Virgos to be guided by their feelings and thus question their routine actions. For example, the Cancer can appeal to the Virgo's sense of compassion when it comes to the suffering of animals in the meat industry, or suggest that the Virgo is not emotionally involved enough with children, partners or friends due to their strict sense of duty.

Cancer and Libra

The Cancer meets the Libra as the tenth sign, so this relationship is a matter of leadership and dominance. Cancers can prove to be very insightful and humane bosses who have a sincere interest in their employees. If a Cancer wants to manipulate a Libra, he only has to appeal to their sense of justice and will thus bring the Libra to take on tasks for which they are not paid or persuade the Libra to take on more responsibility than they actually have to. The Libra is ideal for taking the rap for others.

Cancer and Scorpio

As the ninth sign, the Cancer may enrich the life of Scorpio a great deal by making the Scorpio familiar with new lessons that can change his worldviews significantly. At the same time, Cancers are also very successful demagogues in the guise of a humble teachers and supporters of absolute truths. It is precisely because the Cancer manages so well to empathize with others and to recognize their needs, he can seduce and alienate the Scorpio ideologically. The Cancer bestows recognition, compassion and understanding. The Scorpio often feels misunderstood and is therefore defenseless against this type of manipulation.

Cancer and Sagittarius

The Sagittarius fears nothing as much as failure and life crises. He will do anything to avoid them and get into a real panic if a failure threatens. The Cancer may support him in his emotional coping of the crisis, but it is also easy for the Cancer to manipulate the Sagittarius once the Cancer has gained the trust of the Sagittarius. The Cancer will convince the Sagittarius of dangers that do not exist and thus move him to action, which cost him a lot of money and only benefit the Cancer.

Cancer and Capricorn

Cancer is the seventh sign for the Capricorn. For the overthinking Capricorn, there is a great attraction to the sensitive Cancer. If the Cancer wants to manipulate the Capricorn, he aims at the often-suppressed feelings of the Capricorn, which the Capricorn considers as a weakness. The Cancer brings the Capricorn to trust him with his most intimate secrets in order to use these against him later.

Cancer and Aquarius

The Aquarius makes compromises for the love of his friends. He does not like to be alone and needs the company of others. The Cancer successfully persuades the Aquarius that he must make numerous concessions in order not to be left alone, which is one of the greatest fears of the Aquarius. The Aquarius knows that he often lacks a deep emotional attachment to his many friends and partners. He is capable of rallying people around him and inspiring them. He gets along well with everyone a superficial level, but deep relationships are rather hard for him. The Cancer may take advantage of this uncertainty and bring the Aquarius to act against his nature, but this does not serve the Aquarius well for long, since he will rebel against it and act cold to the Cancer.

Cancer and Pisces

Cancer and Pisces are both water signs, so they have a lot in common. Feelings play a major role for them. A collaboration promises creative successes and a friendship can be very deep and intimate. The Cancer may manipulate the Pisces by persuading him to ascribe his feelings even more importance than he already does. The Cancer confirms to the Pisces even the most irrational emotion and reinforces this. Thus the Pisces loses touch with reality all too easily and can lose himself in obsessions and delusions.

Cancer and Aries

The Aries will always prefer to put their head through the wall. The Cancer recognizes this impulse and will hold the Aries back from them by asking him questions like: "What would your father say?" or "How could you do that to your mother?" In this way, the Cancer slows down the Aries and forces him to keep himself in check. This can be positive, but can also make the Aries into a toothless tiger that is alienated from his own nature.

Cancer and Taurus

Cancer is the third sign for the Taurus. The great strength of Cancer is that he listens very carefully. Reading between the lines, Cancer reads hidden longings and fears. It is precisely these that the Cancer will use against the Taurus when he tries to manipulate him. For example, the Cancer can incite the Taurus to jealous behavior by persuading him that his partner would flirt with others and thus destroy the relationship.

Cancer and Gemini

The Cancer meets the Gemini as its second sign. Actually, the Gemini does not place much value on material items, but it is part of the manipulation by the Cancer to abandon this attitude, at least temporarily. The Cancer will use the right arguments, such as the safeguarding of their own family or the fear of an accident, to bring the Gemini to invest money for financial security and insurance.

5. How the Leo manipulates

The Leo is brimming with power. He is bold, loud and likes to be the leader. But he expects recognition and allegiance. He needs the company of others in order to feel well, but only on his terms. He can also achieve this by means of manipulation, although the Leo actually prefers a direct confrontation. Sincerity and honesty have high value for him and he will always prefer to attack directly than to try tricks. Therefore, attempts at manipulation are easier for Leos to detect than other signs. As a sign of the fifth house, he stands for creativity, joy, fun and the sunny side of life. For him, life is a stage on which it is necessary to present yourself.

Leo and Leo

Two Leos can respect each other, but usually a group can only accommodate one person with this zodiac sign. If a Leo is daring enough to manipulate another Leo, he will challenge him to a real competition for attention. Which of the two is the more generous? Who can gather more friends around? Inspire more women or men for themselves? This contest will tie up all capacities of the other Leo and soon wear him out.

104

Leo and Virgo

For the Virgo, the Leo is the 12th sign and literally arouses primal fears in the Virgo. She is afraid of being eaten by him, of being devoured together with skin and hair. The Leo takes advantage of this fear by intimidating the Virgo both verbally and physically. The Virgo does not like to be in the spotlight. Too much attention unsettles them. The Leo puts the Virgo under enormous pressure with his loud roar. His presence is often uncomfortable for the Virgo, though the Virgo does not know why.

Leo and Libra

The Leo meets the Libra as the 11th sign. The two combine their pronounced sense of humor and sociability so they are often good friends. The Libra does not mind that the Leo always has to be the focus of attention so they rarely get in each other's way.

Leo and Scorpio

Leos can be very unpleasant bosses. The Scorpios know to sing songs about this. But because Leos are so susceptible to flattery, in this respect it is usually the Scorpios who manipulate the Leos. They know as employees or subordinates they can only lose in open battle with the Leo, so they act subtly and in the background.

Leo and Sagittarius

Meaningfulness, the motto of the ninth sign, has great significance for the Sagittarius. He is happy to instruct others, but does not like to be taught himself. This can lead to conflicts with the Leo. However, the Leo has enough self-confidence to insist on his point of view and thus incite the Sagittarius to expand his own knowledge horizon through the encounter with the Leo.

Leo and Capricorn

Through his determination and his diligence, the Capricorn does everything possible to avoid crises. In the process, he often neglects the affairs of the heart. If the Capricorn meets the Leo, he often experiences that his feelings forge new paths in an uncontrolled manner, which is fueled by the behavior of the Leo. The Leo will bring the Capricorn to lose sight of his goals and to become entangled in emotional matters that can ultimately result in a painful defeat both professionally and privately. The very pronounced desire of the Leo acts like a drug on the Capricorn, which he cannot escape.

Leo and Aquarius

In this connection, two opposite zodiac signs encounter each other and have exactly this contradictory effect on each other. It is hard to determine who has the greater manipulative force on the other, because they desire each other and have an almost irresistible attraction to each other. The Leo can manipulate the Aquarius by constantly putting him in the shadows or involving him in loud, public disputes, which are very uncomfortable for the Aquarius. The mutual attraction can turn into sudden rejection if feels one of them feels cheated by the other. Typical accusations of the Leo to the Aquarius are: "You just want my money" or "Without me you're nothing."

Leo and Pisces

The Leo cannot do much here. He admires the Pisces for his kind and compassionate way. It is not difficult for the Pisces to compromise, but in the encounter with its sixth sign, the Leo, too much is demanded of him. All alleged compromises in reality only serve the Leo. Because of the Leo's diverse needs, he will demand this compromise with a vehemence, which the Pisces can do nothing against and will take more and more space in a relationship than he is willing to concede the partner.

Leo and Aries

It's party time! This could be the motto of this relationship. Together, Leo and Aries make the night unsafe or embark on world travel. In each other, they will find exactly those companions they need for their adventure. But the Leo has an advantage over the Aries: His force of attraction to others is greater than that of the Aries and he will make the Aries feel this at every opportunity. He will not withdraw out of consideration.

Leo and Taurus

The Taurus is the more tradition-conscious person in this relationship. For this reason, it is rather difficult for the Leo to manipulate the Taurus at this level. If the Leo wants to manipulate the Taurus, then he will outstrip the Taurus from his closest relatives and friends, so that the Taurus almost gets beside himself with jealousy. Quite naturally, the Leo will pretend to be a family member, and thus touch on the sorest point of the Taurus.

Leo and Gemini

At the communicative level, the Gemini is actually superior to the Leo. If the Leo wants to manipulate the Gemini, he simply has to take the bull by the horns. He will take advantage of the contradictions of the Gemini and demonstrate this to him downright. For example, he will point out to him during a discussion: "But yesterday you were of this and this view" and thus deny Gemini the possibility of considering differentiated things and even being ambivalent, which is one of the great strengths of the Gemini. The Leo will nail him to a stance and interpret any deviation from it as an argumentative weakness.

Leo and Cancer

For Cancer, Leo is the second sign. Material values serve to highlight the Leo's status. He likes to have money in order to spend it again for everyone to see. The Cancer is in its essence a true materialist, which is why it likes to be caught by the Leo. In addition, the Cancer attaches great importance to feelings. The Leo will manipulate the Cancer by devaluing these values repeatedly and even making them ridiculous, which can greatly unsettle the Cancer.

6. How the Virgo manipulates

Virgos are rationally controlled people with a great sense of order and organizational skills. They do not like to lose track of a situation and show themselves as responsible and reliable. In dealing with others, they are often reluctant, but this should not be confused with weakness. They like to explore situations before they act. They find it easy to understand the intentions of others, which is why they also have a knack for manipulation. The Virgo is the sixth sign, which symbolizes everything that has to do with coping with everyday life: work, home, bill payment, insurance, personal care, maintaining health, social obligations and taxes.

Virgo and Virgo

This relationship is paradise for both people. Nothing disrupts their routine and their order. The repetitive processes provide security. At the same time, this characterizes the manipulative power of the first sign. Living means development and growth and both can only take place if one is willing to think beyond rigid order and habit. A virgin can solidify the other in their development by implicating them in a fallacy of affirmation and self-righteousness.

Virgo and Libra

For the Libra, the Virgo is a mysterious creature. The Libra admires the Virgo's sense of order and their expertness. The Libra all too happily resorts to the Virgo as a consultant in all vital questions and listens without protest to their instructions, a position that the Virgo willingly exploits. All the while, the Virgo believes that this is only for the benefit of the Libra. There is a risk that the Libra will become dependent.

Virgo and Scorpio

The Scorpio encounters the Virgo as the eleventh sign. In fact, people of these two signs like to become friends. If the Virgo wants to manipulate the Scorpio, she knows to suggest poison to him about his other friends until the Scorpio strikes out blindly.

Virgo and Sagittarius

Virgos can be very stressful as supervisors. They supervise the execution of duties in a nit-picking manner and have no tolerance for error. If they want to manipulate the Sagittarius, they just need to tickle his sense of honor. For example, if the Sagittarius sees himself as an expert or specialist in a particular area, it will affect him greatly if the Virgo suggests someone else for a corresponding task. He will work twice as hard to prove his superior suitability.

Virgo and Capricorn

For Capricorn, the Virgo is the ninth sign. Both love to keep order and pursue goals. Therefore, the encounter may result in a fruitful and very lasting partnership or cooperation. The manipulative potential of the Virgo on the Capricorn is based on the stubbornness of the Capricorn, which the Virgo effortlessly recognizes as his weakness. The Virgo will know how to set the Capricorn on a specific track, from which he will no longer deviate, regardless of how great the headwind. This gives the Virgo a free hand to portray themselves as more successful and popular.

Virgo and Aquarius

The Virgo as the eighth sign symbolizes for the Aquarius everything he fails at: Order, continuity, fixed procedures. The Aquarius can thus learn a lot from an encounter with a Virgo if he is willing to accept advice from the Virgo. But because the Aquarius is not able to bring order to his life on his own, this is a great gateway for manipulation by the Virgo. In a crisis moment, the Virgo can take complete control over the life of the Aquarius and justifying this by the Aquarius's own inability.

Virgo and Pisces

The emotionality of the Pisces has a confusing and attractive effect on the Virgo. Although Virgos do not like going into uncharted waters, the Pisces get them to make an exception. The Virgo can manipulate the Pisces by causing them to look at things no longer by feeling, but rather only from the perspective of order. For example, they will convince the Pisces that it is more important to stick to a certain routine than to follow a feeling.

Virgo and Aries

Traditions give the Virgo security. They are part of the order within which they like to move. Because the Aries is their eighth sign, Aries' manipulative force is stronger on the Virgo than vice versa. Virgo can try to manipulate the Aries by confusing him with remarks such as "People don't do that" or "What will people think?"

Virgo and Taurus

For the Taurus, the Virgo is the fifth sign. The Virgo will be happy to choose a Taurus as its partner and both will complement each other. If the Virgo wants to manipulate the Taurus, it will insist on order and rituals without any compromise, which will wear down the Taurus over time.

Virgo and Gemini

When it comes to order, the Virgo makes no compromises. But the Gemini leaves the Virgo no choice, if only because as Virgo's tenth sign the Gemini often occurs as their superior. The moodiness of Gemini gets the Virgo out of their rhythm. The Virgo can, however, trick the Gemini by learning to introduce a system, even in his unpredictability, and always being one step ahead, for example, by making it clear what the triggers are for the changing moods of the Gemini and how to change them.

Virgo and Cancer

Harmony and mutual understanding are important to the Cancer. Because the Cancer knows how much the Virgo relies on their fixed routines, the Cancer concedes them to the Virgo, even if this aspect is less important to the Cancer. This makes it easy for the Virgo to manipulate the Cancer and to therefore place their own needs over those of the Cancer. If the Cancer does not meet the Virgo's expectations, the Virgo will accuse the Cancer, for example, in a partnership that he does not love the Virgo, but would rather a) take out the trash more often or b) sweep the stairs.

Virgo and Leo

The Virgo knows that money is very important for the Leo, if only because he can impress others with it. The Virgo will skillfully exploit this weakness in order to manipulate the Leo for their own purposes. The Virgo will entice the Leo with money so that the Leo behaves according to the Virgo's ideas or spoil the Leo with expensive gifts.

7. How the Libra manipulates

Libras have a strong sense of justice. They cannot endure when others are wronged and take personal responsibility to ensure that the injustice is fought. Harmony with the environment is particularly important to them. Consciously manipulating another human contradicts the sense of justice of the Libra, but if the manipulation serves to restore harmony, then they are absolutely willing to take these measures. Libras have a balancing character so that their influence on other people is often rather positive. They stand for the seventh sign, which is about partnerships and attraction, but also love of art. An important issue for the Libra is to recognize themselves in the mirror of others or to provide a mirror to others.

Libra and Libra

As always with the first sign, this relationship is characterized by harmony. Beauty, goodness and truth in life important are important to both and they abhor disputes and conflicts. But conflicts cannot always be avoided and it is important to confront these also. A Libra can manipulate others by leading them to avoid conflicts until they can no longer be solved.

Libra and Scorpio

For the Scorpio, the Libra is the 12th sign. The Scorpio moves for no conflict and may even be vindictive. The Scorpio can learn from the Libra to abandon these impulses. Since the Libra is the Scorpio's 12th sign, the Libra can very easily manipulate him. The Scorpio does not understand the Libra's desire for harmony and balance, but the Libra can give the Scorpio the feeling that the Libra's behavior is better and more successful. A typical sentence in this constellation is: "Do you always have to start an argument with everyone?"

Libra and Sagittarius

The Libra encounters Sagittarius as the eleventh sign. So it is not surprising that they can get along with each other and even be friends. Moral issues and his own sense of honor are important to the Sagittarius, which may be consistent with the pursuit of justice. If the Libra wants to manipulate the Sagittarius, the Libra will present to him moral decay, even where there is none, which means that the Sagittarius will get excited in front of others and appear as self-righteous.

Libra and Capricorn

When it comes to business relationships, Libra and Capricorn work well together. The Libra values the reliability of the Capricorn and the Capricorn in turn values the Libra's sense of justice. However, the Libra can manipulate the Capricorn by constantly comparing the Capricorn with others and holding out the prospect of numerous awards and promotions. The Capricorn will do everything to achieve this.

Libra and Aquarius

For the Aquarius, the Libra is the ninth sign. The relationship between these two signs is therefore about knowledge expansion. Due to the fact that Aquarius is an air sign, the Aquarius has a good attitude towards it and loves boundless discussions and exchanges of views. The Libra can take advantage of this by feigning interest in order to flatter the Aquarius and to therefore learn more about him.

Libra and Pisces

External problems such as financial worries, layoffs or an illness of a loved one throw the Pisces into a deep crisis from which they have a hard time helping themselves get out of. The Libra can help the Pisces to rediscover the inner compass and to get them on their feet, but they can also manipulate the Pisces by representing the situation as more dramatic than it is. Thus the Pisces will turn to the Libra for help and willingly do what the Libra says.

Libra and Aries

The two are the seventh sign for each other, a relationship that is characterized by great force of attraction. Therefore it is very important in this connection for the Libra to establish harmony. However, if the Libra wants to manipulate the Aries, the Libra does this because they want to teach the Aries a lesson to not always tear ahead. One such means is to suggest an idea to the Aries with which he tries to put himself at the center of attention, but inevitably ends up on his nose.

Libra and Taurus

The manipulative power of the Taurus on the Libra is stronger than the other way around, but the Libra can get the Taurus to become more efficient and adaptable in many matters in order to meet their need for harmony. For example, Libra encourages the Taurus to give up certain aspects of his way of life and to slow down and enjoy things. The Libra can also encourage the Taurus to stand up more for matters and to take the side of justice, although this is not necessarily the cause of the Taurus.

Libra and Gemini

The Gemini inspires and spurs on the Libra. The Gemini leads the Libra to discover new areas of interest and to fulfill themselves creatively. A Libra can influence a Gemini by pretending to be a willing protégé who literally soaks up fresh impulses only to then devalue and criticize these ideas.

Libra and Cancer

For Cancer, Libra is the fourth sign. For Cancer, Libra embodies traditional and conservative behavior. For Cancer as a hermit, these values have a high priority, which the Libra skillfully knows how to use for themselves. The Libra plays with the fears of the Cancer of emotional injuries. The Libra can therefore tell the Cancer, for example, that certain things should be done one way or another in order to not have others pitted against him or to not hurt their feelings and as the only legitimacy put forward that as just always been the way of doing things, which is an argument of great persuasiveness.

Libra and Leo

In the field of communication, the Libra is resoundingly superior to the Leo. The Libra knows the rules of successful communication and will specifically use them to restrain the exuberant temperament of the Leo. Language is a powerful tool and choice of words, tone of voice and content determine how we react to spoken word. Thus the Libra will deliberately diminish and downplay events that excite the Leo or even completely conceal them.

Libra and Virgo

Libra and Virgo often go into business together, as they complement each other well. The power of the Virgo over the Libra is greater than the reverse, which does not mean that the Libra cannot influence the Virgo. The Libra utilizes the fact that Virgos are reluctant to give up their familiar workflows. The Libra can intercept unpleasant disruptions and thus make themselves indispensable to the Virgo.

8. How the Scorpio manipulates

Scorpions are very passionate people who embody the principle "all or nothing". They cannot bear ambiguity, nuance or hypocrisies. They fight, if need be, to the death so that the truth comes to light and others take a stand. It is no surprise then that they preside over the eighth house of the zodiac. Encounters with them are a particular challenge for each zodiac sign, because Scorpios put their cherished principles and practices to the test.

Scorpio and Scorpio

As always with the first sign, there is a deep mutual understanding here and an ideological agreement. Unfortunately, this is not always enough to establish a harmonious relationship between two Scorpios. Because both require absolute sincerity and are hardly diplomatic, it can cause serious conflicts. One Scorpio manipulates the other by either breaking through his reserve by consciously betraying him - the worst offense for the Scorpio, for whom there is either all or nothing, friend or foe - or irritating his combativeness so that the Scorpio gets lost in senseless and nerve-wracking conflicts.

Scorpio and Libra

For the Libra, the Scorpio is the second sign. They meet on the material level of self-esteem, ownership and the need for security. This is about roots in the tangible world. Material possessions are not very important for the Libra. Spiritual and aesthetic values are more important to the Libra. Yet Libras have an often well-hidden, great need for security when it comes to their physical environment. If Scorpios wants to manipulate the Libra, this is exactly where they start. The Scorpio lay out scenarios that threaten the Libra's sense of the security, talks about money problems with the Libra that do not exist and builds on the Libra's inability to tackle problems in a specific manner.

Scorpio and Virgo

Virgos are distinguished by their seriousness and strength of purpose. They like to learn, but not for the sake of learning, rather because they are pursuing a goal. They dislike redundant communication, such as small talk. The Scorpio can manipulate the Virgo by getting them involved in open communication battles, preferably in front of audiences. The Virgo abhors embarking into uncertain terrain and is unprepared to fall into such situations. But the Scorpio can also have a positive impact on the Virgo by teaching them the desire to learn for the sake of learning.

Scorpio and Leo

The Scorpio encounters the Leo as the fourth sign. This is about family and origin. The Leo's family is very important to him. He likes to be generous and a strong protector. However, in return he also demands loyalty and recognition. If the Scorpio wants to manipulate the Leo, he challenges the Leo's instincts to protect the family honor. The Leo cannot do anything other than accept this challenge. Due to his hot temperament, however, the Leo is often inferior to the conflict-experienced Scorpio. The Scorpio succeeds in spurring on the Leo until close friends and relatives refuse him allegiance, which saddens the Leo deeply and claws away at his self-worth.

Scorpio and Cancer

The Cancer is the fifth sign for the Scorpio. They meet on a terrain whether neither always feel quite well. It is about socializing, the joy of life and pleasure, but also about the superficial. The Scorpio is suspicious of relationships of this nature, because they have too much ambiguity. The Cancer can fully enjoy the relationships, but quick and superficial friendships are not the right thing for the Cancer. The Cancer looks for in-depth and lasting relationships with others. If the Scorpio wants to manipulate the Cancer, then the Scorpio isolates the Cancer from acquaintances and casual friendships by claiming that these are all marked by hypocrisy and superficiality. This is due to the Scorpio's inability to recognize that contact with other people is about more than just friend or foe, black or white, but that there are real nuances. Furthermore, the Scorpio can manipulate the Cancer by reinforcing the Cancer's tendency to lose themselves in fantasy worlds and pipe dreams, thus abandoning the view of reality.

Scorpio and Gemini

Geminis are characterized by a high mental agility and enjoying thinking. The same old and often arduous demands of everyday life are repugnant to the Gemini. The reality of life between breadwinning, housekeeping and obligations often appears banal and confining to him. At the same time, however, the Gemini knows that his life is often characterized by a lack of direction and a lack of strength of purpose. The Scorpio can convey to the Gemini that the solution to these problems is found in focusing on managing everyday problems. The Scorpio thus robs the Gemini of his mental agility and the strength to think in large contexts and even in a visionary manner.

Scorpio and Taurus

Scorpio and Taurus are the seventh sign to each respectively. Sparks definitely fly between the two, especially on a sexual level. However, the combativeness of the Scorpio is slightly too much for the Taurus. If the Scorpio wants to manipulate the Taurus, he incites jealousy, implicated him in unpredictable debates and thus plunges the Taurus into an emotional mess. It takes some effort to entice the good-natured Taurus from his reserve, but the Scorpio succeeds at this.

Scorpio and Aries

For the Aries, Scorpio is the eighth sign and therefore the one with the largest manipulative force on him. The Aries likes to tear ahead and hates being condemned to inaction. The Aries likes to tackle problems directly and can only rarely be confident that they will solve themselves. The Scorpio as a manipulator reinforces this tendency. But rash actions can exacerbate problems even further, rather than solve them, and sometimes-diplomatic action is the right action, but the Scorpio and Aries are incapable of this.

Scorpio and Pisces

Pisces are characterized by their sensitivity and their uniformity. While they have their views on topics such as religion and philosophy, it is not important for them to enforce them in disputes. It is precisely this differentiation that is contrary to the opinions of the Scorpio. This can result in a corresponding conflict on the one hand and, on the other, the withdrawal of Pisces from the Scorpio, since the Scorpio's brash attitude is alien to the Pisces. The Scorpio may succeed in manipulating the Pisces by reinterpreting the Pisces' reservation in matters of faith and religion as cowardly and isolate the Pisces this way. For the Pisces, isolation is the worst punishment and an effective means of manipulation.

Scorpio and Aquarius

Aquariuses love extremes. They want to enjoy life fully with all its ups and downs. Freedom is a great commodity for the Aquarius. And professionally, they need a lot of space and find it rather difficult to subordinate themselves. Scorpios again can be very dominant superiors, whether at work, in associations or in politics. If they want to manipulate the Aquarius as such, they only need to overwhelm him with meaningless tasks, which he is required to accomplish on account of the ruling hierarchy. The Aquarius will soon give up and look into the distance.

Scorpio and Capricorn

Good partnerships and friendships are formed between Scorpios and Capricorn because they are evenly matched. However, the Capricorn has the advantage over the Scorpio: The Capricorn is more businesslike and level-headed and does not act easily from emotion. Capricorns carefully choose the battles to which they commit. The Scorpio, however, can only rarely resist a dispute and is passionate in conflicts. If Scorpio and Capricorn decide to cooperate, it may result in some success, but only if the Capricorn succeeds in taming the Scorpio. This is quite possible in a friendship. As the eleventh sign for the Capricorn, the Scorpio can bring the Capricorn to judge other people not only by their performance, but also to accept them as they are. If the Scorpio tries to manipulate the Capricorn, the Scorpio will make use of the fact that self-discipline and diligence take precedence for the Capricorn. The Scorpio will pretend to be a friend of Capricorn and make this work for him by admiring the Capricorn for his achievements and explaining to him that nobody could cope with certain tasks as well as the Capricorn.

Scorpio and Sagittarius

The Scorpio is the twelfth sign for the Sagittarius. The Sagittarius admires the Scorpio for its unwillingness to compromise and because when Scorpios are in doubt, they do not care what others think about them. His personal reputation and position in society are of great importance for the Sagittarius. Sagittarius tends to idealize his relationships with other people. Therefore, it is not easy for him to see through the Scorpio who is trying to manipulate him. The Scorpio has good cards when giving the Sagittarius the impression that, because of his adherence to principles, he has the right to be hurtful and inconsiderate toward others,

The manipulative abilities of the various signs of the zodiac

a tendency that has already been created in the very nature of the Sagittarius and can be exacerbated even further by the Scorpio.

9. How the Sagittarius manipulates

Sagittarians are very active people who especially like to prove themselves in intellectual challenges. Adherence to principles and recognition are very important to them. They tend to be impulsive and idealize, but are also generous and dedicated to diverse interests. The ninth house, which they represent, stands for spiritual ideals, for the study of philosophy, morality and religion. "What constitutes ethically correct action?" or "Am I a good person?" are typical questions that the Sagittarius asks himself.

Sagittarius and Sagittarius

Sagittarius and Sagittarius come together as like-minded people. Everyone recognizes themselves in others. It is easy here to also idealize the relationship and yourself, thereby losing grip. They quickly talk each other into the fact that no one else acts more morally correct then themselves and thus justify a superior to condescending action towards others. If a Sagittarius intends to manipulate someone, the easiest way to do this is to give this person the ranking as a moral compass in a group, a family or a business. The other Sagittarius will not take this humiliation of his self-esteem lightly.

Sagittarius and Capricorn

For Capricorn, the Sagittarius is the 12th sign. As always in this constellation, it deals with a mysterious force of attraction, spirituality and engagement with last things. The Capricorn will find the energetic Sagittarius and his moral conviction fascinating, because for himself is it rather difficult to ride into battle on a principle. Also questions of faith and spirituality play a rather secondary role for the Capricorn. The Sagittarius can get the Capricorn to deal with these aspects of life. However, the Capricorn leaves the terrain of certain facts and clear answers that is important to him, which confuses him and makes him vulnerable to deception. The Sagittarius can now be a guru to the Capricorn who is superior to him in all spiritual questions and be a spiritual leader to the Capricorn, where the floodgates are open to him for any manipulation.

Sagittarius and Aquarius

The influence of the Sagittarius on the Aquarius as its eleventh sign is low, because this is about the topic of friendship, which is also the dominant theme in the house of Aquarius. At the same time it is about the ideals, hopes and dreams of a future better. In the field of ideals, Sagittarius and Aquarius often meet as like-minded people. The Sagittarius often occurs as a supporter of the Aquarius in his concerns and helps him with money or contacts. Herein lies the key to manipulation of the Aquarius by the Sagittarius: The Aquarius will feel obliged out of gratitude to favors that actually go against him.

Sagittarius and Pisces

Because of their disposition, professional ambition is rather remote to the Pisces. They strive for solidarity and harmony with other people and have no competitive thought on the day. They put themselves in others' shoes and are therefore prevented from acting against their interests. It is therefore only too easy for the Sagittarius be able to manipulate the Pisces so that they no longer pursue their own path and do all their work in the service of the Sagittarius. The Sagittarius can appeal to the helpfulness of the Pisces, such as with statements like "I cannot make it without you" or "I need you." At the same time, the Sagittarius may rest assured that the Pisces would rather avoid a conflict with the Sagittarius and therefore give up the pursuit of his own objectives. If the Sagittarius therefore threatens the Pisces with a dispute or a discontinuation of communication, he will be able to almost always prevail.

Sagittarius and Aries

The Sagittarius has a particularly strong impact on the Aries, because this is about the area that best corresponds to his essence: conviction, religion and philosophy. Aries is often too impatient to deal with these aspects of life. Contact with a Sagittarius can enrich his life greatly in this respect, but the Sagittarius can also abuse the temperament of Aries to help resolve conflicts while the Sagittarius himself prefers to remain in the background. In this way, the reputation of the Sagittarius in society receives harm, while the Aries often does carry some injuries without understanding at all exactly what happened to him. Manipulation can be such that the Sagittarius presents an actual or alleged injustice dramatically to the Aries and brings the Aries to punish the perpetrator.

Sagittarius and Taurus

Radical changes and breaks are not for the Taurus. The Taurus pursues its objectives judiciously without overworking. The Taurus relies on stability and serenity. Nevertheless, the Taurus also cannot avoid having to face existential questions in life, whether it be money worries, illness, death of close relatives or other cuts. The Aries can learn from the Sagittarius that it is useful in such situations to turn to faith or a certain philosophy in order to discover a meaning in the crisis experienced. In this devotion is already hidden the gateway for the manipulation of the Sagittarius, because he waits patiently until the otherwise strong Taurus is in a wounded and already ailing situation and directs him with false promises into a direction that actually goes against the thoughts and actions of the Taurus.

Sagittarius and Gemini

Sagittarius is the seventh sign for the Gemini. As always in relation to the seventh sign, there is a benevolent force of attraction between the two from which a successful cooperation can arise. The Sagittarius will turn out to be the more down-to-earth person in these relationships and thus maintain the trust of the Gemini. Within this trust, he can freely tap into the wealth of ideas of the Gemini and display them as his own.

Sagittarius and Cancer

The effect of a Cancer on a Sagittarius is greater than vice versa, because the Cancer is the eighth sign for the Sagittarius and the Sagittarius is the sixth sign for the Cancer. Nevertheless, there are also manipulation possibilities in this constellation. The Sagittarius can get the Cancer to sacrifice themselves for him, to care for him without regard to himself and to relieve him of all everyday adversities. The Cancer does not frivolously enter into relationships with other people, so that the Sagittarius has to invest some time and energy to build a close relationship with the Cancer, but once succeeded, it is very difficult for the Cancer to get out of this relationship that is disadvantageous for them.

Sagittarius and Leo

Sagittarius and Leo recognize and appreciate each other. In a mutual exchange, there is plenty of room for inspiration, traveling together and expanding of horizons. Here the Sagittarius can learn from Leo that one "you can let things slide for awhile" as it is popularly said. Creativity, play and love of life are areas that the Leo knows well and feels at home and is therefore not easily susceptible to manipulation. However, the Sagittarius can be successful in this regard by deliberately spoiling the fun for the Leo, such as with moral admonitions. Nothing kills a party more reliably than to remind someone at the height of the high times how much suffering there is in the world at the same time, thus reminding the partiers of own their ignorance. It is exactly this weapon that the Sagittarius will use when wanting to manipulate the Leo.

Sagittarius and Virgo

Their origin and a close relationship with their family are of fundamental importance to the Virgo. This satisfies their need for simplicity and predictability as well as the protection of their privacy. As their fourth sign, if the Sagittarius sets out to manipulate the Virgo, the Sagittarius will alienate the Virgo from its family in a targeted manner. Virgos are responsible and reliable people who both take care of their own children as well as their parents. The Sagittarius will mislead the Virgo to no longer consider this as part of their responsibility and to neglect their duties. In this way, conflicts with the family are inevitable, which upset the life plan of the Virgo.

The manipulative abilities of the various signs of the zodiac

Sagittarius and Libra

Justice is very important to both the Sagittarius and the Libra. For the Sagittarius, this is above all an immaterial value, which he defends with philosophical arguments, while the Libra deals with it in a more practical manner. If a Sagittarius wants to manipulate a Libra, the Sagittarius will try to confuse the moral compass of the Libra through grandiose arguments. The Sagittarius will persuade the sensitive Libra through endless debates to generally question their own life choices and appearance to others, thus losing self-confidence.

Sagittarius and Scorpio

For the Sagittarius, the Scorpio is the 12th sign. Reversed, the Sagittarius is the second sign for the Scorpio. The influence of the Sagittarius on the Scorpio is therefore often less than the other way around, but there are also possibilities for manipulation in this constellation. When Scorpios feel challenged, they sting figuratively. It is of no consequence to them whether they have to fear financial losses as a consequence of their behavior or the loss of important business contacts. If the Sagittarius would like to hurt the Scorpio, the Sagittarius has only to fuel this behavior and the

Scorpio will act accordingly. A suggestion here suffices that a roommate lied, that a long-time colleague of his is slandering him and already the Scorpio will confront both of them, argue with them or even break off contact.

10. How the Capricorn manipulates

Professional success, personal excellence and self-discipline are especially important for the Capricorn. The Capricorn is determined and ambitious. The Capricorn sometimes tends to lose sight of the finer things in life throughout all of the work and learning. Capricorns can incite other people to perform better and are very good as an appropriate role model. The tenth house, which the Capricorn represents, deals with career success, ambition and almost dogged pursuit of set objectives. Capricorns are born superiors who are tirelessly good role models.

Capricorn and Capricorn

As the first sign, they can be allies and bitter rivals. A Capricorn values the motivation and determination of the other. As long they both have areas clearly separated from each other and mutually ensure their respect and their appreciation, everything is fine. However, if a Capricorn gets wind that the other Capricorn could outdo him, he will move on to the attack and start an open competition, which can take on grotesqueness. Capricorns often have little understanding of the inefficiency of other people and expect them to be at an equally high level of performance as they

143

themselves are. Therefore, friendships between two Capricorns can reinforce their tendency towards independence and discipline. If one Capricorn wants to manipulate the other, he challenges him in the competitive struggles described above so that he lacks resources for other projects, or both seclude themselves as supposed elites from other people who henceforth view the Capricorn with distrust and defense.

Capricorn and Aquarius

It is not easy for the visionary Aquarius to understand the level-headed Capricorn. The Aquarius respects and admires the Capricorn for his strength of purpose and ambition. At the same time, the Capricorn's tendency towards fun hostility is suspect to the Aquarius. The Aquarius wants to be close and share with others, while the Capricorn rather shuns distractions of this kind. If a Capricorn wants to manipulate an Aquarius, the Capricorn aims to convince the Aquarius that his quest for spiritual fulfillment, for connectedness with other living beings and horizon-expanding experiences is nonsense, with which the Aquarius shies away from growing up and taking responsibility. The Aquarius knows that exactly this is one of his weaknesses.

The manipulative abilities of the various signs of the zodiac

An Aquarius will take a closer look at itself and feel caught and make an effort to rise again in the favor of the Capricorn.

Capricorn and Pisces

Capricorn and Pisces could not be more different. Where the Capricorn is ambitious and hardworking, the Pisces is dreamy and prefers to be carried away by the flow of life. Professional success and the achievement of objectives mean everything to the Capricorn, but the Pisces lives in his own world of dreams and desires. The relationship between the Capricorn and Pisces can be very fruitful, because by the encounter with the Capricorn the Pisces gets a better grip on reality and their needs. The Capricorn, by contrast, learns to use control for once and to resign to life. If a Capricorn wants to manipulate a person with the zodiac sign Pisces, then he will specifically attack the dream worlds of the Pisces, which cannot withstand a matter-of-fact examination, but are of vital importance for the Pisces. The Capricorn will draw the image of reality for the Pisces that is full of efforts and sacrifices and that is not created for the Pisces. In reality, the Capricorn is distinguished in this case only by his own perception, which in turn is only one aspect of reality, but the Pisces tends to take this view and to find himself incapable of surviving in this view. An even stronger escape from reality in the form of drugs, alcohol or dreams may be the result.

Capricorn and Aries

The Capricorn is a born boss, leader or political leader. Its effect on the Aries is particularly strong for this reason. At the same time, it is difficult to the Capricorn to understand and accept the impulsive Aries so that there is often friction between them. The Capricorn manages to manipulate the Aries by consistently devaluing his professional services and, because of his impulsiveness and the impetuous approach, denying him the ability to accept responsibility or to climb up the career ladder.

Capricorn and Taurus

The deprivation-rich efforts of the Capricorn are rather suspect to the Taurus. For the Taurus, life is characterized by wealth and abundance. For this reason, the Capricorn and Taurus can get in ideological discussions together, because they follow two very different philosophies. The potential manipulation of the Capricorn over the Taurus is to exploit its penchant for mental laziness and to offer him supposedly simple answers to complex situations. In this way, the Capricorn can talk and act as a pied piper who makes the Taurus into a fellow traveler.

Capricorn and Gemini

The Capricorn meets the Gemini as the eighth sign. The dominant themes of their encounter are existential questions about procreation, birth, death, illness, money, destruction, as well as renewal and growth. The Gemini is prone to crises, because he himself is never quite sure. The Gemini suspects unknown abysses both inside him as well as in others. Gemini's always live with the feeling that they cannot rely on themselves entirely and expect ambivalence to self-destructive behavior from themselves. The discipline of the Capricorn can be a way for him to control these tendencies, but to really dominate them he must look into these abysses. If the Capricorn is set on manipulating the Gemini, he accelerates this process without adapting the pace to the needs of the Gemini. To meet his own dark side, a certain degree of stability and inner strength is needed, otherwise there is a risk of surrendering to it and completely deviating from the path. If this is missing in Gemini's and they are still tirelessly urged by Capricorn to deal with themselves, a collapse is almost inevitable.

Capricorn and Cancer

The Capricorn can hardly start dealing with the emotionality of the Cancer. Emotions play a subordinate role in his life. Since Capricorn and Cancer are the seventh sign for each other, they can only rarely meet neutrally. Either they feel a strong force of attraction or an intuitive dislike for the other. Due to their essential difference, partnerships do not last long, because the Cancer cannot live with the emotional coldness of Capricorn. The Capricorn in turn cannot live with the emotional outbursts of the Cancer. For the Cancer, his feelings reflect reality. The objective point of view, which the Capricorn uses, is foreign to the Cancer. The Capricorn can manipulate the Cancer by constantly relativizing his feelings and perception, depriving the Cancer of them and even making fun of them.

Capricorn and Leo

Little also connects these two. The Leo likes to be the center of attention. Arduous work in the background that is necessary to achieve goals is not his thing. Quite different from the Capricorn, who goes his way away from the great turmoil and persistently sticks to it. He does not need recognition by others. The achievement of his objectives is confirmation enough for him. Since the Capricorn is the sixth sign of the Leo, he has the power to force the Leo to compromise and behave pragmatically. The Leo loves to be on the sunny side of life and flees from the dark and gray sides. The Capricorn may succeed in downright taming the Leo by repeatedly prompting him to be more ambitious and disciplined. Endurance is not one of the strengths of the Leo, so he fritters away his powers and loses his radiance.

Capricorn and Virgo

Capricorn and Virgo understand each other well. Both are ambitious and success-oriented. The Capricorn appreciates the Virgo's organizational skills and reliability. The Virgo appreciates the Capricorn's ambition and determination. Both are more down-to-earth characters and do not need great emotional upheavals nor the limelight. Cooperation is usually topped by long-standing and long-term success. If the Capricorn wants to manipulate the Virgo, he takes advantage of the Virgo's dependence on manageable processes, which he deliberately destroys through sudden changes, new requirements or shortened time limits. Thus the Virgo loses the ground under their feet and soon feels useless and incompetent.

Capricorn and Libra

The Capricorn experiences the Libra as an indecisive to fickle character. To the Libra, it is important to bring yourself in line with the world and other people. The Libra does not want any no sharp demarcations or conflicts. The Capricorn meets the Virgo as a fourth sign as a perpetual admonisher of tradition and origins. The Capricorn will make reproaches to the Virgo if they surround themselves with people who do not share the values of the canon of the Virgo family and drive this in front of the Virgo in their indecision. The Capricorn's justification for this intrusive behavior relates to the traditional values and conceptions, which the Capricorn internalizes and applies with ease. They are part of his recipe for success, because he likes relies on the tried and tested. In a typical manipulation conversation between a Capricorn and a Libra, the Capricorn will dismiss the friends of the Libra as "good-for-nothings" and maybe even "failures."

Capricorn and Scorpio

The level-headed Capricorn will immediately recognize that the Scorpio closes so many doors with its uncompromising all-or-nothing attitude, can be all too often engaged in meaningless fights and thus will not do its own goals justice. Because as a latent outsider the Capricorn is classified as a very keen observer, he will use this vulnerability for himself if it wants to manipulate the Scorpio. The Capricorn will get the Scorpio to start disputes where there are none and thus little by little clear him out of the way as a potential competitor.

Capricorn and Sagittarius

The Sagittarius fights like a noble knight for truth and good, for his principles and beliefs. He may also become a tragic figure, because for other people these aspects of life are less important than for himself. Although he claims that substantive concerns are less important to him than the ideal concerns, the Sagittarius still has a great need for security. The Capricorn, however, certainly measures its success in the accumulation of material goods, which he does not have to flaunt. The Capricorn knows the dark side of life very well and is ready for it. That is part of its appeal to the Sagittarius and makes the Sagittarius prone to manipulation by the Capricorn.

11. How the Aquarius manipulates

As an air sign, the Aquarius has little grip in the material world. Its terrain is the spiritual world, the world of ideas and visions. Often an Aquarius has a large network around them, supporting the Aquarius and admiring him for his inventiveness, without there being a real emotional friendship connecting him to these people. No ideology and no thought construct are alien to him and he loves dealing with the questions about the meaning of life. The eleventh house, which he represents, therefore is also under the sign of friendship and intellectual exchange. Competition, jealousy and deceitfulness have little space here. It is much more about achieving something together and having a good time. But it is precisely because the Aquarius often seems quite harmless that he can manipulate others.

Aquarius and Aquarius

Aquarius and Aquarius recognize themselves in each other. It lies at the essence of Aquarius to deliberately enter into friendships under the aspect of personal advantage for himself that rarely have two Aquariuses in one circle of friends. The Aquarius prefers to take more than he gives and does so with a naturalness that makes it hard to criticize him for it. His behavior towards others has something childish or playful about it. The Aquarius does not like discovering such behavior in another person at all and he will put up a fight against these competitors by highlighting his own value to the circle of friends and depreciating the other person, for example, because he himself hosts the best parties, is the more ingenious scientist, the more popular scene experts or experienced specialist. The Aquarius will not shy away from personal insults.

Aquarius and Pisces

For the Pisces, the Aquarius is the 12th sign. The Aquarius's manipulative effect on the Pisces is essential, because the Pisces admires the Aquarius's quick-witted intellect. The boundless imagination and individuality of the Aquarius appears very mysterious and interesting to the Pisces. The Aquarius has an opportunity to manipulate the Pisces when he opposes what the Pisces believes in with scientific evidence. Thus the Aquarius often contests the Pisces's naive philosophies of life and views and cites numerous examples for this purpose. In this way, the Aquarius manages to desecrate the mysteriousness and to deprive the Pisces of his magic, which represents an existential threat to the Pisces.

The manipulative abilities of the various signs of the zodiac

Aquarius and Aries

The Aries meets the Aquarius as the eleventh sign. The crucial aspects of their encounter, namely friendship, visions, hopes and new ideas, mean a home game for the Aquarius. For this reason, the Aquarius has a greater manipulative effect on the Aries than vice versa. Since the Aquarius in principle accepts other people as they are, the irascible temperament of the Aries gives the Aquarius no trouble. For a manipulative perspective, however, the Aquarius manages to put the Aries in front of his own cart, for example to make him have unpleasant conversations or to blame him for all sorts of events. Because the Aquarius is all too happy to remain in the field of ideas, he wants rarely take responsibility for practical action. It is exactly this responsibility that he transfers to the Aries by explaining that this is part of the common breakdown or is important for a project.

Aquarius and Taurus

The Aquarius is only suitable to a limited extent as a supervisor and leader. While he can proceed with his ideas and visions, he has nothing to do with the practical tasks of a boss or lead manager. The Aquarius does not want to control his staff or bother them with pesky organizational issues. The more leisurely Taurus as his subordinate embodies everything for the Aquarius that makes leadership so exhausting. For this reason, the Aquarius will treat the Taurus unfairly and perhaps even downright bully him. The Aquarius will make the Taurus responsible for errors, for which the Taurus had nothing to do with and the Aquarius will expose the Taurus in front of others. Here the Aquarius benefits from the good nature of the Taurus.

Aquarius and Gemini

The Gemini is very open to what the Aquarius offers him. The Gemini is interested in new ideas and is committed to the realization of a better world. This impact is reinforced by the fact that the Aquarius is the ninth sign for the Gemini and in this context deals with the expansion of the mental horizon. The Aquarius manages to manipulate the Gemini, because the Gemini hopes to get final answers from the Aquarius to the questions that have bothered him, namely "Who am I?" and "Why am I here?" The Aquarius has a whole range of responses to these questions, but no general validity. Due to his inner turmoil, the Gemini will only be able to hardly grapple with these non-binding statements, because he is looking for certainty. For a time, however, the great range of ideas and insights that the Aquarius offers will have a great force of attraction on the Gemini.

Aquarius and Cancer

For the Cancer, the Aquarius is the eighth sign and for this reason has the greatest manipulative force on the Cancer. Cancers know no hardness, neither inside against themselves nor outside against others. Sometimes they put up protective armor in the course of their life, but they strip off time and time again. They are prone to emotional injuries and manipulations. The Aquarius often appears to them as a seducer who recognizes their most intimate desires and needs and takes advantage of this. Frequently proximity and sexuality play a role. Too often it is also about the need of the Cancer to be in a state of emotional security. However, the security offered by the Aquarius is deceptive. The Aquarius only knows his own needs and cannot do anything with the feeling-rich world of the Cancer. A life with him is a life of uncertainty and emotional capriciousness.

Aquarius and Leo

Aquarius and Leo fall in love with each other easily. Together, they make the perfect pair, one is loud and bright, generous and confident, the other full of intellectual wit and surrounded by many friends. There is a risk that the two are more in love with the idea of themselves as a couple and their impact on the outside and are not necessarily in love with each other. Their world is often marked by beautiful appearance and lacks grip and depth. If the illusion shatters, hateful wars of roses and absurd rivalries are often the result. The respective person aims to destroy the other and erase the memory of him or her. The Aquarius will reproach the Leo that he, like every human being, also has less radiant days, perhaps even has fears and self-doubt. For the Aquarius, this amounts to a kind of fraud, which he will also reproach the Leo with.

Aquarius and Virgo

Since the Virgo is the eighth sign for the Aquarius, the Virgo's effect on him is stronger than vice versa. Nevertheless, the Aquarius may succeed in manipulating the Virgo and indeed precisely where the Virgo supposedly knows best: in the field of daily obligations and numerous concessions that daily life brings to us. The Aquarius will make fun of the Virgo's adherence to rigid procedures and blame the Virgo's lack of imagination, call them boring and predictable.

Aquarius and Libra

Libras strive to keep everything in balance. The encounter with an Aquarius can be invigorating and inspiring for the Libra, but they both together crave a better world in harmony and balance. The Libra's need for harmony, however, is greater than that of Aquarius, so that the Libra will often give in for the sake of love of peace, even the Aquarius is stuck on a recognizably crazy idea. The Aquarius manages to inspire the Libra with his suggestions and make the Libra into an energetic combatant. Together, they can make a big difference. However, the Libras cannot protect themselves from being drawn into financial escapades and ill-conceived projects by the Aquarius.

Aquarius and Scorpio

The statement that something is not so because "it has always been done this way" does not suffice for the Scorpio.

He wants absolute truths and unambiguous answers. The Aquarius succeeds extremely well in enticing the Scorpio to conflicts with family or old friends by repeatedly questioning their views and countering with new and supposedly more fresh ideas. Tradition does not need any more legitimacy than that it is just tradition. It does not need to be logical nor particularly efficient or equitable. Their existence is justified by the time period in which it took effect and that continues to the present. The Scorpio cannot and does not want to be satisfied with such a statement, although he presumably was never actively thinking about his origins and the associated traditions until an Aquarius prompted him. The Aquarius can bring the Scorpio to go into open opposition to the expectations and unwritten laws of their own family and so entirely renounce them. The Aquarius will especially cite rational arguments here, which do not consider that tradition and origin as well as the entire range of conservative thought have a lot to do with emotional attachment.

Aquarius and Sagittarius

For the Sagittarius, the Aquarius is the third sign. In their encounter, it is all about human contact with each other, about exchange of information, discussions and communication. The Sagittarius is often described as a stickler for his principles who is wordy in communicating with others. His weakness is that he rarely rethinks principles that were once adopted as correct and clings to them with remarkable obstinacy. The Sagittarius lacks the skills to take a completely different point of view or to respect others' opinions, both of which are great strengths of the Aquarius. For this reason, the Aquarius succeeds in cornering the Sagittarius in discussions and showing others the Sagittarius's stubbornness and obstinacy, which is to the detriment of the Sagittarius and his public image.

Aquarius and Capricorn

The Capricorn encounters the Aquarius as the second sign. So it is no wonder that these two frequently argue about money, that the Aquarius spends too frivolously, which the Capricorn worries too much about. If the Aquarius wants to manipulate the Capricorn, then he only has to use his natural ability to get others to pay for him. The Aquarius will explain to the Capricorn that he has invested his money poorly or simply that he is in dire straights and the Capricorn will step in begrudgingly. The Capricorn will have the impression that the Aquarius simply lacks seriousness and vision so that he is almost innocent in this situation.

12. How the Pisces manipulates

Pisces stand for the deep, unfathomable and mysterious. They are very sensitive, both in terms of their own suffering as well as with respect to the suffering of others. Their desire is to go with the flow and avoid all obstacles. They are true masters of unconscious manipulation. This is namely their innate ability, which they use very often and often cannot help it. Their house is the 12th house of the psyche and this is about everything that cannot be seen with the naked eye, what we only feel, guess and suspect. The Pisces is at home in this world, which makes most other people rather afraid.

Pisces and Pisces

The other zodiac signs often find it difficult to understand the Pisces. It is all the more pleasant for them to meet other Pisces, with whom they can share their penchant for the supernatural and transcendent in tacit agreement. They shy away from the practical demands of life. Pisces can manipulate each other insofar as they support each other in their latent denial of reality. Not all conflicts can be avoided. Sometimes it is urgently necessary to take a position. Problems do not disappear if you ignore them. Pisces can be whisked away into a dream world that has nothing to do with reality. Drugs or other addictions can also play a role here. To outsiders, this dream world cannot be understood and they also have no access to it.

Pisces and Aries

For the Aries, the Pisces are the 12th sign. The elusive persistence of the Pisces is alien to the Aries. The Aries prefers to actively storm ahead. An Aries too often runs with his head against the wall, appears stubborn and breaks up formalities. If the Pisces wants to manipulate the Aries, the Pisces needs do nothing else than avoid the Aries's ill-considered and hasty attacks with a short fin stroke. The Aries needs clearly identifiable enemies who adopt a position and offer themselves as targets. By Pisces avoiding exactly this, they irritate the Aries and let him run around with his horns until he is completely exhausted.

Pisces and Taurus

The Taurus is not easily fazed. For the Pisces, he is often the much-described safe haven. But even the calmest contemporary only has limited potential to endure influences. Just as a stone will be sanded down in the long run by the water, the Pisces will subtly and persistently change the Taurus so that he no longer recognizes himself. Fully in line with their nature, they avoid debates and clearly identifiable actions. Rather, they use very subtle stimuli. They give the Taurus proximity when the Taurus behaves in accordance with their wishes and punish him with distance if he differs from the Pisces's wishes. The Pisces seduces the Taurus silently and through gestures. But the Pisces never lets it come to an open quarrel or recognizable discord.

Pisces and Gemini

Guiding others and the assumption of responsibility is not for the Pisces. For this reason, they are also rarely encountered as superiors. As part of a subtle manipulation, the Pisces can make use of the tendency of the Gemini to always listen with just half an ear and not being able to concentrate for long.

Pisces and Cancer

Both the Pisces as well as the Cancer are characterized by their sensitivity and compassion. Both like to believe in the paranormal and find meaning in it for their daily lives. While this world is truly real for the Pisces, the bond of the Cancer to it rather consists of a love for all things traditional, old, mythical and legendary that give him a sense of home and familiarity. It is easy for the Pisces to obtain the trust of the Cancer, because Cancers have the feeling that they can better understand their own origins through the Pisces. The easiest way for the Pisces to manipulate the Cancer is to offer himself to the Cancer as a medium that talks to him about and interprets sensory experiences.

Pisces and Leo

The Leo is completely rooted even in this world, here and now. No wonder then that the Pisces, with their penchant for the transcendental, are secretive and mysterious to the Leo. However, everyone strives for balance in their interior so that even the Leo instinctively senses that important things await him in the encounter with the Pisces. The Leo escapes from the inner contemplation through extravagant parties and excessive self-presentation. Often his thoughts and actions are marked by superficiality.

The manipulative abilities of the various signs
of the zodiac

Pisces and Virgo

A tactile attraction rules between Pisces and Virgo. The
order of the Virgo gives the sensitive Pisces security, but it
can also quickly constrict the Pisces. The Virgo feels
accepted and understood by the Pisces. In the best case, this
contact can result in an intimate relationship or friendship.
If the Pisces wants to manipulate the Virgo, they talk the
Virgo into it being necessary to "just drop things," to enter
into the unknown, spiritual and incomprehensible. But the
Virgo needs firm ground under their feet and will react to
this with great uncertainty and self-doubt.

Pisces and Libra

When people of these two signs meet, nobody feels quite
well. The Libra always strives for balance between the
extremes of different views and characters. The Pisces with
their sensitivity and their penchant for dreaming embody an
extreme. Reliability, accuracy and attachment to material is
not their thing. The Libra know, however, that these aspects
are necessary for a successful and happy life If the Pisces
deliberately sets out to influence a Libra, then it is necessary
to destroy this balance. They keep the Libra from producing
this balance with daydreaming, with inaction and even with

the consumption of intoxicating substances. The Pisces can live in the chaos that arises from this, while the Libra cannot.

Pisces and Scorpio

The Pisces are the fifth sign for the Scorpio. The Scorpio gets along better with the Pisces than inversely. The Scorpio finds the dreamy and sensitive attitude reassuring. This is precisely where the manipulation potential of this relationship lies. The Pisces can have a downright soporific effect on the Scorpio who wants to appear to the world with new plans and ideas. Through subtle tricks and deceptions, the Pisces can keep the Scorpio from the concrete realization of his plans, so that the Scorpio, just like the Pisces, becomes the eternal dreamer. This means that the Pisces impedes compliance with important business dates or successfully isolates the Scorpio from other people who could be important for his plan.

Pisces and Sagittarius

Sagittarians are idealists. This is also reflected in the relationship with their families. Either they idealize the relationship, their own childhood and education or they have turned away from the parents and their values as a disappointment, because they did not find this good enough. In this idealization or devaluation is a great deal of vulnerability, because both do not correspond with the truth and it requires mechanisms of repression in order to maintain it. This is where the manipulation of Pisces comes into play. They talk with the Sagittarius about childhood memories and remind him of painful truths. This may result in feeling of guilt, but also fear of abandonment and depression.

Pisces and Capricorn

The Pisces are the third sign for the Capricorn. Their encounter deals with communication, a knowledge transfer and lifelong learning. It is difficult for the Capricorn to understand the Pisces and their rather sluggish action. The reveries and the ambiguity of the Pisces are alien to the Capricorn. The Pisces can succeed in manipulating the Capricorn by constantly drawing him into discussions, meetings and other encounters on the emotional level rather than the factual level. Thus, compassion, feelings of guilt, childhood memories, complexes and moral obligations are appealed to and even tears are used to prevent the Capricorn from implementing their goals.

Pisces and Aquarius

The manipulative power of this combination is not very strong. The Pisces are the second sign for the Aquarius. For the Aquarius, their contact is marked by the topics of material possessions, money and security. For both signs, these aspects do not play a major role. Nevertheless, the Pisces can influence the Aquarius by bringing him to provide the Pisces with material possessions. The Pisces can appear as helpless, sick and weak and appeal to the compassion of the Aquarius. At least for a while, the Aquarius will be manipulated in this way.

III. The targeted manipulation of the different zodiac signs

In part II, we learned how each zodiac sign influences others. This last part is about how to deliberately manipulate a particular zodiac sign. As already mentioned in the preface, I give this knowledge only for the sake of completeness on and strongly advise against ever using it against other people except in an urgent emergency. Above all, it is intended for you to be able to detect and avert such manipulations at an early stage. Everything is interconnected in our universe. Every action causes a variety of reactions that are often not straightforward, similar to a domino effect. Surely you have heard that a single butterfly flutter can trigger a storm. This saying symbolizes that nothing in our world can be viewed in isolation and separated from its environment. So if you choose to deliberately manipulate another human being, then it may be that this manipulation has a negative effect on you in the end. Behind a manipulation intention is a negative energy that always returns like a boomerang to the one who emits it.

Nevertheless, it is one of the platitudes that the world does not just consist of good and considerate people. On the contrary: We treat each other as competitors and all too often an attempt is made to manipulate the will of another.

This is done in a job by colleagues and superiors, in a partnership and among friends by means of advertising, news and by the environment in which we act. Each of us is manipulated, whether we like this realization or not. It is all the more important to clearly remember this fact. In the moment when we realize that and how someone is manipulating us, it loses its effect on us. For this reason, I will hereafter go into detail on how to manipulate individual zodiac signs. Under your own zodiac sign you will find many references in which you will recognize yourself and at the same time identify potential manipulators in your environment.

1. How to manipulate an Aries

Aries are the first sign in the zodiac circle. They symbolize the beginning of spring, the awakening of nature, impetuous growth and an unbridled will to live. They are the representatives of the first house, which stands for self-awareness and a healthy selfishness for self-assertion in the world. You can imagine the Aries as a newborn child who proclaims with a loud cry that it has arrived in the world. The top priorities are their own needs and the perception of the world from their own perspective. A child cannot do a lot of thinking about the consequences of their own actions, because he lacks the experience for it. That makes him bold, curious and fearless. Aries are therefore very spontaneous and often even behave naive, especially when someone has gained their trust. Since they themselves do not take hypocrisies and lies into account, it is difficult for them to recognize and understand that other people very likely do this.

The great strength potential of the Aries exists for a reason. As the first sign in the course of the year, the Aries meets the other zodiac sign in their territory, namely under the auspices of those aspects that characterize the homes of the respective signs. The Aquarius is the eleventh sign for the Aries and therefore has an influence over the Aries in terms of the "friendship," which is also one of the dominant themes of the eleventh house, presided over by the Aquarius. This means that the manipulative effect of other signs on the Aries is even greater. The Aries' weapons against this manipulation are his courage, his honesty and his irrepressible zest for action, which distinguishes him from all other signs. The Aries does not hesitate, he acts. This is his great advantage.

People with the sign of Scorpio have the greatest manipulative force on an Aries. They are the eighth sign for the Aries. The Aries does not like to think about profound truths. He gladly throws himself into new challenges and has a tendency to be impatient. In the encounter with a Scorpio, he meets someone who embodies a very different stage of life or season. The Scorpio stands for death in the fall, the approaching winter, the end of growth, cold, retreat and the fight for survival. Scorpios are secretive and determined, they distrust life because of many relevant experiences and are characterized by a great stamina. These traits are not only strange to the Aries, but it is impossible for Aries to understand them. For Aries, life is rich, exuberant and full of possibilities. The Scorpio is able to give this joy of living a toxic aftertaste. The Scorpio can constantly warn the Aries of risks that make him despondent and make him doubt himself. An Aries who is afraid of the potential downsides of life will lose their vitality and thus an essential feature of their character.

Alternatively, the Scorpio can urge the Aries to tear ahead imprudently and to risk their neck with careless talk. Under the manipulation of Scorpio, Aries will argue with people who would be important for his professional advancement. He will shut doors instead of building bridges and stand alone in the end.

But other zodiac signs can certainly achieve a great manipulative force on the Aries. For individuals who themselves are Aries or belong to the signs of Leo and Libra, this is likely to not be a big problem. You can excellently incite the Aries to tear ahead on sensitive matters while you stay in the background. If, for example, you are dealing with the implementation of a new project with the supervisor, simply explain to the Aries that he is the best person for the task because of his strength and position. That would be the path that the Sagittarius would choose if he wants to manipulate the Aries.

If you as an Aries want to manipulate another Aries, always appeal to his usually slightly exorbitant self-image. The Aries will hardly be able to resist. If you yourself are an Aries, then you are urgently on the lookout when another person repeatedly praises you to the skies and constantly affirms everything you do. They could be hiding something else behind it. Do not fight battles for others that are not your own! Choose well when a struggle is worthwhile for you and when it only benefits others. The Libra, Virgo and Leo choose this way of manipulating. You can also give the feeling to the Aries that others are making fun of him or that he constantly alienates people by his lack of tact and appears as an uncouth bumpkin.

The Capricorn, however, will deny the Aries what he needs most: praise and appreciation of his performance. The Capricorn will point out to the Aries that he is not looking ahead and therefore is not suitable to take over responsible tasks.

Aries have a zest for action. They are impulsive, energetic, agile and dynamic, and show a great initiative. Therefore, as employees, they are quite outstanding. It is not one of their strength to think for a long time about the consequences of their actions, so that it is useful to provide the Aries with a Virgo or Capricorn who takes this task over for him. As friends and partners, they are quick to jump into the breach for others and are therefore liable to be used by others in this way. The quickest way to manipulate an Aries is flattery and praise.

2. How to manipulate a Taurus

The season of the Taurus is in the spring, in May. Everything is green and nature is in abundance. Absence and fear have no place here. On the contrary, the Taurus stands for material security and enjoyment. The Taurus is characterized by patience, perseverance, a love for harmony and peace, and the finer things in life. Material possessions, prosperity and coziness characterize his life and also the 2nd house of the zodiac, over which he presides. Justice and prudence are typical of his character.

The Taurus is not prone to rash decisions and does not enter into deep friendships quickly or enter into a partnership recklessly. But if you have won his confidence, he is a lifetime loyal friend and partner and is loyal, reliable and predictable. Separations hit him deeply, because once he has made a decision, he sticks with is. The Taurus does not have arbitrary emotional outbursts. The Taurus is more leisurely and constant. This can easily fall into a penchant for convenience, which is also a starting point for manipulation, such as the jealousy of the Taurus or his lack of mental agility.

The Sagittarius has the largest manipulative effect on the Taurus as his eighth sign. Like any other human being, the Taurus is also not immune from crises and setbacks, but

177

often lacks flexibility in his ideas and actions to be able to deal with these crises properly. The Taurus has to realize that his past behavior no longer works and reorient himself, which is precisely one of his weaknesses. If a Taurus is in a real or even perceived crisis, such as of a financial or professional nature or after a separation, then Sagittarians have a particularly easy game with the Taurus. They offer the Taurus comfort in the form of philosophy and religion, but this consolation is more a refuge than a solution to the tangible problems. A Sagittarius can then establish himself as a kind of moral or religious leader, perhaps by means of questionable esoteric methods, giving the Taurus the feeling of being able to overlook his situation better.

Gemini, Aquarius and Capricorn apply both in the mental immobility of the Taurus. It is not as if the Taurus lacked intellect, he is simply too comfortable to think more than he needs to. As long as something works, the Taurus sees no need to get lost in spiritual heights. Both the Gemini and Aquarius as well as the Capricorn can manipulate the Taurus by directly or indirectly persuading him he is too stupid to recognize or understand nuances. The Capricorn will offer the Taurus supposedly simple answers so that the Taurus is not forced to think for himself. Gemini and Aquarius will mock the Taurus.

Another weak point of the Taurus is his sensitivity. The Taurus loves creature comforts of all kinds: good food, travel, massages and sex. The Taurus is very easily seduced here, of which the Cancer, Aries and Scorpio know to take advantage. Especially in relation to sex, it is easy to literally turn the Taurus's head and to seduce him into risky, frivolous and immoral acts if one provides him great sexual pleasure or knows how to skillfully satisfy his desires. The Taurus is happy to be ready to return the favor, also in a material sense.

Since the Taurus himself is very loyal and values stable relationships, he tends to be jealous. It is important to understand that the Taurus is not easily fazed. For a long time the Taurus will take what happens to him in a good nature until he finally lashes out with all his strength. In such moments, the consequences of his actions do not matter so that a continuous aim to make him jealous will ultimately be successful.

As the Taurus's 12th sign, the Aries is mysterious to the Taurus. The Taurus lacks the vitality and impulsiveness of Aries, which at the same time fascinates and irritates him. The Aries can exploit this for himself, because his reliability is far less pronounced than that of the Taurus. Since the Taurus takes reliability for granted, he will not expect that a colleague, friend or partner will simply leave him in the lurch and will be deeply affected by such behavior. This makes it possible to manipulate the Taurus's relationships with others as well as his decisions.

Cancer and Leo both know two secrets of the Taurus. Firstly, the Taurus craves security and safety, a place where he can even be weak. On the other hand, his family and loyal friends are very important to the Taurus and he would do anything to protect them. Both secrets reveal starting points for possible manipulation. Even petty orders not for the Taurus and can propel him to incandescence. Another person with the same zodiac sign can manipulate the Taurus by driving his penchant for coziness to the extreme and thus make the Taurus miss important activities.

So if you as a Taurus are experiencing that someone offers you simple answers to complex issues, turns your head with the breathtaking art of seduction and expects material considerations in return, if you are constantly living in fear in a partnership that your partner is cheating on you, then it is very likely that you are being manipulated. The same is true if you feel silly and stupid all the sudden in the presence of certain people. Once you realize this behavior, it is up to you to protect yourself against it. Remember your strengths and the people around you that you can rely on.

3. How to manipulate a Gemini

In the cycle of the seasons, Gemini represent a time in which the spring, warmth, and the sun have finally gained the upper hand over winter. There's no place for cares or troubles here - instead, everything is pleasant and easy. These characteristics also mark the nature of a Gemini. Geminis are highly gregarious, very outgoing with others, and extremely tolerant. Their motto is "live and let live," and they reject black and white thinking. This can, however, mean that it is sometimes difficult for them to take a stand when it's necessary. Others often say that people whose zodiac sign is Gemini don't have their own opinions. Gemini is the sign of the third house. It is focused on communication, contact, travel, learning, and collecting new experiences. Geminis are distinguished by their high level of intellectual flexibility. Their thinking can change directions quickly, which can also cause them to change their views and statements very rapidly.

At the same time, Geminis are rooted in the spiritual world, unlike Aries and Taurus. Even if they aren't always deep thinkers, they are still concerned with the most important questions in life. They have learned that there may not be clear answers to many of these, and are ready to accept the fact that some questions may have multiple contradictory answers. Geminis know that every question has more than one side, and their greatest strength is seeing the big picture and taking a sophisticated view of the issues. Their job is collecting and transmitting information, and this is where they truly shine in life. That's why they make excellent mediators. But Geminis also have weaknesses. Their inconstancy and lack of reliability can make them difficult partners, whether professionally or in personal relationships. They need variety, and are always looking for something new. Loyalty isn't exactly one of their distinguishing characteristics.

People with other signs need clarity, and they might not understand that Geminis are comfortable thinking in more of a "both, and" manner, rather than "either, or." This also applies to their world view, religious leanings, and other opinions. Geminis don't know where they want to go in life, and lack determination. They aren't able to concentrate well, and often don't listen closely. Others see them as erratic and driven by an inner sense of unrest. Geminis exude this unrest because they are running away from themselves. They don't want to look into their own depths, out of fear for what they will find there. That's why they avoid Inner reflection, peace and quiet, and structure like the devil avoids holy water.

Capricorn, as its eighth sign, embodies exactly the opposite. Capricorns never lose the ground under their feet, don't let themselves be led astray, and are ambitious, clear, and goal-oriented. The Capricorn's decisiveness gives him a clear advantage over Geminis. Capricorns can hold a mirror up to Geminis without compromise, and interpret their characteristic fickleness as a character flaw. They will show Geminis that their restlessness is a way of running away from themselves and of avoiding growing up. If Geminis face a crisis of any kind, they will be especially susceptible to this type of manipulation. Capricorns can encourage Geminis to get involved in self-destructive behaviors or to see them as saviors in a time of crisis, causing Geminis to see themselves as bound to them for life. This is the kind of obligation Geminis avoid.

Taurus can have a similar manipulative influence. With their leisurely manner, they can have a crippling influence on volatile Geminis. They will continuously admonish Geminis to get involved in binding financial obligations like rental agreements, insurance, or purchasing a car, since these are part of growing up. The Gemini, however, avoids these kinds of obligations because he knows how unreliable he can be. Geminis don't take care of their own material security or that of their families, meaning they are continuously thrown into situations in which they must rely on the help of others. Virgo and Scorpio can also take advantage of this weakness.

Leo can take advantage of the inconsistency that Geminis display to the outside world, since Leos emphasize and point out this inconsistency to others, causing Geminis to be met with mistrust and distancing behavior. Leo uses the Gemini's restless nature, as do Libra, Cancer, Aquarius, and Pisces. Anyone who wants to manipulate a Gemini only needs to entice him with something new, exciting, or never seen before to get him to throw his supposed friends and acquaintances under the bus. Geminis are unable to resist this temptation. Other Geminis can also use this weakness, often in combination with shielding the manipulated Gemini from all other influences.

If you are a Gemini yourself, then you should be on guard if someone wants to use new activities and ideas to entice you to give up something you know and trust. Security and stability shouldn't just be seen as characteristics of smugness and coming to a standstill, but as necessary supports for a stable and successful life. The attractive power of new ideas must be carefully weighed against their consequences. Be careful that others don't see your behavior as inconsistent and unreliable. Exude reliability, and don't be afraid to show your true colors when you need to.

4. How to manipulate a Cancer

Cancer is the first zodiac sign of summer. Cancers are characterized by mildness and softness. They let their feelings guide them in all matters, and don't use intellectual analyses as the basis for their decisions. Cancers are characterized by high levels of compassion, sympathy, and helpfulness. These aspects make them susceptible to manipulation. Their disposition makes them easy to influence. They are emotional and easily injured. They react quickly by withdrawing, and don't like to try new things. They love antiques and whatever's tried and true, and are definitely focused on family, since they are intensely interested in their ancestry and origins.

These topics are also characteristic for the fourth house, in which Cancer presides. Religion and the esoteric can play a large role in their lives, however, Cancers tend to hold on to their convictions almost fanatically, and are only rarely prepared to reflect on their views.

Cancers feel where others think, and in doing so can easily forget that feelings aren't objective, but instead the result of our upbringing and previous life experiences. Often, it is necessary to examine feelings and reactions to determine whether they are appropriate in view of actual facts or whether they will remain permanent. Cancers often lack this ability almost entirely. They may have no ability to perceive the world objectively at all, but rather see everything through the lens of their feelings. Feelings, however, are easily to manipulate, allowing others to influence Cancers to their own advantage.

Aquarius, as the eighth sign, has the greatest manipulative effect on Cancer. Aquarius recognizes Cancer's longing for safety and emotional security and toys with it. Aquarius can threaten to leave Cancer in a crisis situation or to exploit Cancer's readiness to help to the point of complete self-abnegation, an approach also taken by Sagittarius and Virgo. Cancer easily develops feelings for others, and can be stirred up into a frenzy if others don't reciprocate these feelings or react to them in an ambivalent manner. They have a difficult time believing that others love them for who they are, so they are ready to undertake major efforts to achieve love and security. Aquarians don't let crisis situations get to them, which is why they can't understand the extent of the emotional uncertainty Cancers say they feel. They can make Cancers feel that they are overreacting, causing Cancers to lose their trust in their own feelings and become helpless.

This is why Cancers should leave themselves options to retreat and protect themselves from emotional injuries. Aries, as the tenth sign, takes away exactly this retreat, driving Cancer away until Cancer gives up, exhausted. Cancers aren't concerned with success, so they don't need to distinguish themselves through constant activity. They are more like sponges, absorbing impulses from other people. Virgos are only all too willing to subject themselves to Cancers, Leo and Sagittarius can emotionally injure Cancers through biting remarks and devaluing their ideals. Capricorns are always attempting to qualify Cancers' perceptions, which are based on feelings. "Don't make such a big deal," or "Don't be so emotional" are classic examples of this type of manipulation, and are similar to manipulation by Aquarius, although they don't have such major effects.

Pisces don't just function as an esoteric medium for Cancers, they also tend to reinforce their inclination to make emotional statements. This can easily turn into a type of egotism in which only their own feelings count.

Volatile Geminis fascinate Cancers greatly, although they react to Geminis' mood swings in a hurt and insulted way. This kind of relationship can quickly turn into emotional dependency, which the Gemini creates with his random fluctuations between closeness and distance – an almost deadly trap for a Cancer.

In general, there are various ways to manipulate a Cancer. Their emotions make them susceptible to being talked into feeling a certain way or to having their feelings qualified. Cancers also react quickly in an injured or offended way. If someone doesn't take their feelings seriously, or even specifically tries to injure their emotions, they will withdraw completely. This is one way to eliminate them as a possible competitor. They have a great longing for security, and family and private life are very important to them. Working on these areas can exploit a Cancer's helpfulness. Other Cancers, especially, can utilize these insights.

If you are a Cancer and feel that other people are always taking you on an emotional rollercoaster, then it's highly likely that these people aren't really interested in you at all. Instead, they are manipulating you using your sign's characteristic weaknesses. Be careful if someone wants to force their way into your family or your safe spaces too quickly, and consider whether your feelings of sympathy can really help you make a decision about another person or are just a projection of your own longing for security. It's good to be there for other people, but never lose sight of your own goals and values.

5. How to manipulate a Leo

In the course of the seasons, Leo signals the start of high summer. The sun is gleaming in the heavens, and anyone who can find a shady spot sits to wait until the heat has passed. Lions, as predatory cats, sleep most of the day. Only when they are hungry do they go on the hunt, returning quickly with their prey. They aren't too interested in strenuous activity, and would prefer to relax. At the same time, they are majestic animals - unmistakable and impressive.

Many of these characteristics are also reflected in the personality of the sign Leo. When they step into a room, they command the attention of everyone in it. They are loud, extroverted, and love to be the center of attention. They prefer to have everything revolve around them. They are firmly convinced that the pure fact that they exist should be enough to garner them universal admiration. They possess great strength, but little endurance, meaning continuous activity isn't one of their strengths. Instead, they tend to give out after they've received the applause they were looking for. Admiration is their bread and butter - they can't exist without it.

They love sun and warmth, and don't have any use for the darker or colder side of life, or for hard work and a low-key existence. They skillfully apply their strengths wherever they can attract the most attention - frequently, this can cause them to overpower others. Leos are generous and courageous. They have a refined protective instinct, and their charisma allows them to inspire and enthrall other people. They are representatives of the 5th house, which is focused on self-expression and creativity.

Anyone who wants to manipulate a Leo can use various aspects of the Leo nature. Their primary aspect is their great need for recognition, praise, and admiration. Geminis and Libras, for example, can use this weakness by involving Leos in intellectual discussions in public, in which they will ultimately appear incompetent and uninformed. The more an audience watches this charade play out, the more effective this will be. For Geminis, everything that has to do with communication feels like a home game, while Libras encounter Leos as the third sign, meaning they have a major manipulative effect in the area of communication. They can also convince Leos that someone is trying to challenge their place in the sun as a leader. Another Leo will take over this role, if they want to manipulate someone with the sign Leo.

Cancer, as the twelfth sign, remains a mystery to Leos. The emotional nuances Cancers easily recognize remain hidden from them. This allows Cancers to either talk Leos into having a bad conscience or to appeal to their generosity.

Leos love to throw money around since this gains them respect, even though they don't necessarily know how to handle money well. They enjoy throwing parties and giving expensive gifts. Virgos can bait them with money, binding them to obligations. This allows them to turn the predator into a toothless, harmless lion, opening him up to ridicule - one of the worst punishments imaginable for a Leo.

Taurus takes a similar approach, often seeing Leos as lame and boring. They are often in positions of authority over Leos. If a Taurus plays his cards right, he can confuse a Leo by alternately praising him and devaluing him, totally independent of the Leo's performance or behavior. This randomness will drive a Leo practically insane.

People with the zodiac sign Capricorn can exploit the Leo's relaxed or even lazy disposition for their own purposes. First, they can create dependency by taking over a difficult task for a Leo, or they can expose Leos to senseless discipline, which will quickly exhaust them and give them no chance to make the grand entrances they love so well.

Aquarians are highly attractive to Leos, and the two can often create very popular couples. However, in many cases neither is able to develop deep or long-lasting feelings. They are too egocentric for this. When this kind of relationship breaks up, Leos usually worry most about their popularity and reputation, which can open them up to blackmail.

People with the zodiac sign Pisces have the greatest influence on Leos.

The Leo, a proud sign, can't handle defeats or setbacks very well. They start to doubt themselves quickly and worry about being made fun of by others. Shame can be a major driver for Leos in crisis situations. In these situations, however, Pisces can offer dubious ways to handle the crisis without losing face.

As absurd as these suggestions might be, Leos will accept them for fear of losing face. Pisces exploit the latent superficiality of Leos, since they only rarely think about transcendental questions, and are ready to believe anything a supposed expert tells them in a crisis situation, as long as it seems helpful to them.

As a Leo, it's important to not let yourself be too dependent on the opinions and respect of others. Your reputation in society isn't everything. Large gifts of money that come with obligations, and people who are ready to offer you their help in taking on troublesome tasks are warning signs: Someone could be trying to manipulate you. Trust your self-confidence and your intuition.

6. How to manipulate a Virgo

The zodiac sign Virgo stands for everything related to order, planning, organization, and systematic thinking. It's no wonder that its season is Indian summer, the time we harvest the fruits of the warm seasons and store them away for the winter. Virgos anticipate the coming cold and the time of deprivation, so they store up reserves.

Through their organization, they try to get a handle on the chaos and avoid as many crises as possible. They also stand for care and precautions, and for the principle of motherhood. They are somber and cautious. It's easy for them to see through other people, although they have a hard time giving anything away to others. They have a hard time dealing with inconsistency. They always need something to do, even if it's just cleaning up and organizing possessions. They act in a proactive manner, and take all possibilities into account so they can be prepared to handle them. Occasionally, this can turn into latent pessimism.

As representatives of the 6th house, Virgos stand for everything that has to do with security in everyday life, for career, daily routine, the household, maintaining health, and parenting. Strong emotions and adventurous ideas don't move Virgos; they focus on taming the uncertainties of life through organization so they can be prepared for any eventuality.

The sign with the biggest influence on them are people with the sign Aries, since this is their eighth sign. The impulsive Aries brings chaos and disorder into the well-ordered life of the Virgo. Like a force of nature, Aries break into their small, introspective worlds. They might represent sexual temptation, or just be good friends. Aries will encourage them to take spontaneous trips or go out partying all night, so they're no longer able to stick to their usual everyday routine. Pedantic Virgos can't handle these deviations very well or react to them in a flexible way; this would make them feel insecure or as if they were losing their grip.

Taurus also tries to influence Virgo through distraction, perhaps through expensive gifts. These can exceed what would be appropriate in the eyes of a Virgo, causing them to feel obligated towards the giver.

People with the zodiac sign Cancer find it easier than others to win the trust of a Virgo. They offer a shoulder to cry on if the everyday battle has been especially tough or if the Virgo doesn't feel he's receiving any thanks for his efforts. Cancers can convince them to be led by their subjective feelings as well as objective considerations.

Leo, as the twelfth sign of Virgo, can seem frightening. Virgos don't like to be in the limelight, and they can see that loud bravado often conceals nothing more than hot air. Nevertheless, Leos can make them feel uncertain and shy; just their presence can often be enough to do so.

Libras, on the other hand, can make themselves invaluable as mediators in upcoming changes, while Scorpios can get Virgos involved in debates that sap needed energy.

The zodiac sign Sagittarius targets an especially sore spot for Virgos: their worry about and care for their families. Family is one of the most important grounding forces in the life of a Virgo. Sagittarius can separate them from their family in a targeted way, stop them from keeping their agreements, or cause them to become forgetful. "Think of yourself now and then!" they will whisper.

Although Capricorn and Virgo actually get along well, Capricorns know that Virgos have a difficult time dealing with sudden changes to agreed procedures. Capricorns can attack exactly this weakness during collaborations of any sort. People with the same sign can encourage Virgo's pedantic behavior to the point that others see them as self-righteous and friendless.

People with the sign Virgo can be successfully manipulated by purposefully bringing chaos into the order they need to survive. Shaking the foundations of their existence, which are preparation, planning, order, organization, and care, can quickly make Virgos feel uncertain or even desperate.

If you're a Virgo, it's a good idea to pay attention to whether people respect your everyday routines or continuously interfere with them, even with seemingly good intentions. These people include those who stop by unannounced, even though they know you're busy, who involve you in discussions, even though you're on the go, and who keep you from being on time to and being prepared for appointments. These people could be intending to manipulate you. The same is true for people who give you expensive gifts and tempt you into spontaneous activities. Spontaneity in and of itself isn't a virtue - it takes a certain type of person. Being spontaneous is difficult for Virgos. It's a good idea to pay attention to your own needs and not let yourself be overpowered. If you make it through the night unprepared, you might have to live with the fact that you won't get much done the next day.

Weigh carefully whether you can handle this kind of compromise, and be certain not to lose yourself in the process.

7. How to manipulate a Libra

In the course of the seasons, the Libra stands for fall, which still brings a few warm and sunny days, even though winter is just around the corner. Overcoming the contradictions between abundance and lack, heat and cold, light and dark takes plenty of adaptation, which is why Libras are masters of adaptiveness. They are always looking for balance, and for common elements. They aren't interested in radical views or in extremes.

For people with the sign Libra, contact to and interaction with other people is vital for their survival. Isolation and loneliness are terrible for them, and very difficult to bear. In general, they focus on the beautiful things in life, such as art, culture, travel, good food, and can even have a penchant for luxury. After all, their sign is still marked by the experience of abundance in the summer.

Libras love to think big, but working through details isn't one of their strengths. They are generous, without wanting to be in the limelight like Leos, for example. Others see Libras as charming and attractive. Just because of who they are, this attractiveness can give them a certain manipulative effect on others. At the same time, their dependency on contact with others is their greatest weakness.

One of their most important characteristics is their clear

sense of justice, which can cause them to speak out against and actively fight injustices, whether they affect them personally or others. This characteristic is based on their tendency to be fair with everyone which, of course, is impossible.

At the same time, Libras are often hesitant and indecisive, because they don't want to tip the scales towards any one side. This can make them slow to react and passive in crisis situations.

As a sign of the zodiac, they characterize the seventh house. This house is focused on attraction, partnership, and harmony. Libras try to learn more about themselves through the mirror of other people. The energies flow, and their focus is on respect and togetherness, instead of withdrawal and isolation.

People with the sign Taurus can have the greatest influence on Libras. Taurus is the eighth sign for Libra. Crisis situations require clear and quick reactions, and decisive action. This is exactly what Libras are lacking, due to their tendency to want to collect knowledge. Taurus can stand by their side with practical suggestions or can even act in their stead. This makes Libras dependent on the favors of Taurus, and susceptible to paternalism by Taurus.

Alternatively, a Taurus can distress a Libra by practically forcing him to make decisions. Libras feel a strong attraction to Aries, but Aries often follow their own plans. Since friendship and trust are so important to Libras, they have a hard time understanding that someone could purposefully misuse trust for their own interests and conceal the truth from them.

Gemini, on the other hand, can misuse Libra's sense of justice, manipulating them into becoming unwilling accomplices in unjust deeds. Cancers also follow this approach, expecting too much of the Libra and calling it a fair distribution of responsibilities. They might act as though they are emotionally unstable, causing Libras to throw themselves into the breach.

Virgos, as the twelfth sign, are hard for Libras to understand. They recognize that Virgo's sense of order can be an advantage for them, and allow them to take control over crucial aspects of their own lives - under the pretext, of course, that doing so is for the good of the Libra.

Libras need constant interaction with others. They can often be found at get-togethers and other places offering lots of opportunity for discussion. This is how Libras shore up their own identities. If you cut Libras off from these social contacts by discrediting them or blackmailing them emotionally - often possible in partnerships - Libras basically fall apart. They are nothing without constant contact to others. The same is true if Libras can't enjoy their love for beautiful things because they run out of money. They quickly feel depressed and discouraged.

In general, Libras aren't able to handle crises well or extremes of any type. In a crisis situation, they can easily lose their balance and be susceptible to insinuations and influences. Other Libras, especially, can entice a Libra to stick their head in the sand, which only makes things worse.

As a Libra, you should be wary of letting others make decisions about your life, no matter how difficult this is for you. This kind of support always comes with a price, and all too often can take on the character of paternalism. You should exercise special caution with people whose sign is Taurus, if they try to force you to make decisions or act for you. Justice is important, but if someone tries to use an injustice to make you act a certain way, you should consider carefully whether that injustice has truly occurred. Maintain your contacts well. They are very important for you - be sure no one comes between you and your friends. If anyone tries to isolate you, it's highly likely that you are being manipulated.

8. How to manipulate a Scorpio

The time of the Scorpio begins at the end of October, an uncomfortable time of year. It gets dark early, fog hides the sun, and it is cold and rainy. Summer is over, as is the golden beauty of early fall. No wonder that this time of year is when we turn to thinking of the past, commemorating the dead and All Saints' Day. This is the time in which we come to understand that death is just as much a part of life as birth.

People with the sign Scorpio are characterized by a strong will, great adaptability, and toughness. They are able to handle crises by completely transforming themselves. They take the cycle of life for what it is, and aren't afraid of its darker side. Scorpios have no interest in superficialities; they want to seek out truth instead. They are decisive, and have great critical thinking skills and an almost inexhaustible will to work.

They don't do anything halfway. Once they've got a goal in mind, they pursue it stubbornly. This is also their weakest point: Once a Scorpio has an idea in mind, he can also be so fixated that he can't let it go, even if it's completely clear that the idea isn't feasible. This means they often lose valuable time trying to accept a new idea, which they then devote themselves to with the same dedication. Scorpios are perfectionists who are always testing out their own

202

boundaries and those of others. They see only "black" and "white," and see nuances as nothing but hypocritical falsehoods.

Once they dedicate themselves to a task, they fight relentlessly. Anyone planning to manipulate a Scorpio should be forewarned: If the Scorpio realizes they are being manipulated, there will be no way to soothe them. Also, they will see through heavy-handed manipulation immediately and punish it accordingly. Scorpios don't give second chances, and excuses won't be any use once you've lost their trust.

They represent the eighth house, concerned with crises of all types. Poverty, sickness, mourning, and loss characterize this house, along with the chance that something new may arise from the experience of crisis, allowing the sufferer to find themselves anew and strip away the old life like a shell which has grown too small.

Scorpions have a difficult time abandoning either an argument or a challenge, and can't stand walking away from a conflict without fighting it out. This is another gateway others can use to manipulate them.

Gemini is the eighth sign for Scorpio, meaning it has the greatest manipulative power over them. At the same time,

Geminis are confronting Scorpios on their home turf: dealing with crises. Scorpios have no fear of crises, since they know their strengths and weaknesses very well, and know who they are. Gemini can be successful in manipulating Scorpios if they get lost in making suggestions, giving the Scorpio no concrete points of attack. If a Gemini and Scorpio are breaking up, for example, the Gemini can infuriate the Scorpio by repeatedly breaking off communications and making vague statements.

On the other hand, as the 12th sign, Libra will interpret Scorpio's decisiveness and belligerence as a weakness. In Libra's mind, Scorpio's search for absolute truth and clear assertions can look like a childish or naive worldview devoid of any understanding of reality. This can cause Scorpios to feel uncertain.

Scorpios feel drawn to Taurus, since this is their 7th sign. The two might have a thrilling sexual relationship, although Scorpios can see Taurus as boring due to their comfortable, down-home nature.

Virgos will easily recognize Scorpios' weaknesses and provoke them to arguments so that, for example, they break off contact with important people and family members. An Aquarian follows a similar approach if he wants to manipulate a Scorpio, primarily by trying to tone down his radical potential and induce him to more conservative goals. Sagittarius will focus more on his professional life.

Cancer and Pisces can have a calming or soothing affect on Scorpio, but they are difficult to nail down to clear positions, which irritates Scorpio. Scorpios need clear statements.

As a Scorpio, you possess the best qualities for protecting yourself from manipulation. You are vigilant, don't like compromises, and seek out the truth in all things. By nature, you are on guard for unwanted influences, and don't like to let others get close to you. There are lots of things about you that you keep secret from everyone. This helps keep you safe. Vigilance is advisable if someone refuses to make clear or binding statements or puts you off. The same is true for people near to you who want to egg you on to argue with other people, especially if there's no chance for reconciliation. Be sure you're the one choosing who you're arguing with, and why.

9. How to manipulate a Sagittarius

Sagittarius is the most idealistic of all the signs. They are always striving towards something higher, something beyond the mere material world. They have an obvious relationship with the season they represent: During this season, the world lies petrified under a blanket of snow, and nature is devoid of new growth. We are left with inner reflection, and a focus on that which can only be found within - in books, discussions, and contemplation.

Sagittarians are deeply moral people. They stick to their principles, unshakeable, and others who prove themselves to be less loyal to their own morals can upset them very much. Everything having to do with religion, ethics, morals, and philosophy is the Sagittarian's core area of interest. He understands these issues and enjoys engaging in passionate discussions on them.

Sagittarians are admonishers, continuously reminding others to act based on their understanding and on their heart, instead of just satisfying basic needs like hunger and thirst. Their minds and their souls demand more, so they seek out what they need in the writings of great thinkers or in halls of philosophical or religious learning.

The targeted manipulation of the different zodiac signs

Sagittarians are proactive, but not steady. They often have brilliant intuition.

As representatives of the 9th house, they are associated with everything having to do with world view, reason, the search for truth, and the expansion of their own house.

The strengths of Sagittarius are also his weaknesses. He is a moral person in a world that all too often acts in an amoral manner. One of the basic questions of human civilization is whether morality stands a chance in our world.

Cancer is the eighth sign for Sagittarius. Sagittarians may have only theoretical answers in crisis situations, which frequently aren't applicable in practice. To get the right job, for instance, it may be necessary to get a competitor out of the way. Ethical behavior, however, might prohibit doing so. Such disputes can thrust Sagittarians into a moral dilemma. Cancers can use the Sagittarian fear of such crises to manipulate them. For instance, they could invent crisis scenarios that don't even exist in order to make it clear to Sagittarians that they can't solve these problems with their internal attitudes. This conflict will be an internal ordeal for the Sagittarius, often resulting on serious self-doubt and uncertainty.

Aries and Taurus will often attempt to weaken the moral integrity of Sagittarius to damage his reputation or undermine his self-image. Actions that entice a Sagittarian to unmoral actions will be successful here, for instance acting under the influence of alcohol or in other weak moments. They will beat themselves up over their own feelings of guilt, and be susceptible to all kinds of influence. Geminis can have success with similar tactics, in convincing Sagittarians to get involved in agreements or business transactions that aren't entirely kosher.

Aquarians can also attack a Sagittarian's social position by skillfully emphasizing his know-it-all nature in discussions with others.

Virgos will challenge Sagittarians by pretending to compete with them, while Capricorns will concern them with material cares.

Scorpios can use the fact that Sagittarians believe their morality gives them the right to expose or harm others. This kind of behavior can isolate Sagittarians. Pisces, on the other hand, will target a Sagittarian's childhood memories, a phase of life in which we don't yet understand moral behavior. The goal here too is undermining a Sagittarian's convictions.

The targeted manipulation of the different zodiac signs

It's not easy for Sagittarians to protect themselves from manipulation. This is primarily because of the dilemma described above, but also due to their moral principles themselves. They let themselves become embroiled all too easily in all kinds of causes, and can bend or even be exposed as hypocrites.

You should be careful of anyone who repeatedly attempts to test your principles or expose them as a sham. These people could be knowingly trying to manipulate you.

Hold fast to your moral integrity, but don't turn into a know-it-all. Everyone has to determine the moral compass for their own lives, and it's important that you give others the freedom to do just that.

The quality of an ethical principle is shown by the effort required to defend it and enforce it in practice. So don't just be a moral person in theory, be one in practice, especially when faced with difficult decisions. Addressing the practical situation doesn't mean you're giving up your principles, as long as you stay true to yourself. Be mindful of whether you are hurting or exposing other people, and don't let yourself be carried away to self-righteous behavior.

10. How to manipulate a Capricorn

Capricorns represent the darkest time in the four seasons. It is cold, only a few hours of daylight brighten the day, and nature has ceased her gifts. This is a time of deprivation and of waiting. Endurance and discipline are required to get though these months and make it through to the spring. People with the zodiac sign Capricorn are somber, goal-oriented, and ambitious. Away from all the hustle and bustle, they pursue their goals and stick to them unrelentingly.

They move confidently even through the most difficult terrain, and stay steady even where others falter. Their whole being is dedicated to their aspirations, they work to gain recognition and honor, and they are difficult to dissuade from their goals. "Now, more than ever" is their motto, as they fight stubbornly against seemingly insurmountable odds. Others often see them as cool and distant. At times they can even seem condescending and domineering.

The 10th house, which they proceed, symbolizes professional success, social respect, and everything associated with career and power.

It is possible to influence a Capricorn by exploiting his ambition, discipline, and goal-oriented nature. Taurus, for example, follows this approach. Because of the relationship between their two houses (Taurus is the 5th sign for Capricorn), Capricorns tend to follow their suggestions. This allows the Taurus to let Capricorns work for him, while he sits back and relaxes. Capricorns feel it is important to complete tasks, and their feeling of obligation means they don't relinquish responsibilities once they've taken them on. Capricorns see themselves as studious and proper, and secretly they feel that no one else is able to complete tasks as well, precisely, and reliably as they can. This makes them susceptible to being used by others.

Scorpio and Virgo can also manipulate Capricorns in this manner. Scorpios act like friends who constantly ask Capricorns for small favors, while Virgos elevate a Capricorn's studiousness and discipline to ends in themselves. They tell Capricorns that other values don't count, and that people who believe in other values are dumb or lazy.

Pisces can manipulate Capricorns by handling every discussion with the Capricorn on an emotional level. Capricorns don't feel comfortable in this terrain, and always try to reach an understanding on a more practical level. Accusations, feelings of guilt, and elevating emotional sensitivities to the level of facts irritate them and make them helpless.

Aquarians can also use helplessness as a successful ploy against Capricorns. They might pretend they don't have their lives organized well enough, or that they aren't able to work regularly and productively, enticing the Capricorn to jump into the breach for them time and again.

Gemini and Cancer can also use the Capricorn's cool emotional spectrum. People with the zodiac sign Capricorn see feelings as a luxury they only rarely allow themselves. If a Gemini wants to manipulate a Capricorn, he might expose him to a firework display of capricious emotions and changing moods. Combined with a lack of reliability and contradictory statements, this can confuse the Capricorn.

Cancers will always appeal directly to a Capricorn's repressed feelings, causing them to come to the surface and throwing the Capricorn off his guard.

Aries can talk Capricorns into feelings of guilt associated with their families. Capricorns don't just have a difficult time allowing themselves to have feelings, but to show them as well. This is why even their closest friends often don't know what they feel or think about them.

Sagittarians often act as a kind of spiritual leader for Capricorns, providing them an oasis of relaxation and ease into which the Capricorn falls, entrusting the Sagittarian with his most closely held secrets.

Leo, as the eighth sign of Capricorn, has the greatest manipulative power over him. Leos can overcome Capricorns by practically overrunning them with wild desires. Capricorns feel themselves drawn to easy-going Leos, who always live on the sunny side of life. However, they also feel a sense of inadequacy because they lack the Leo's levity and popularity. Leos can take advantage of this fact. A Capricorn can force another Capricorn into a relationship of unrelenting competition.

As a Capricorn, you must protect yourself from others who want to use your strengths as a way to manipulate you. Studiousness and ambition are important, but they are only meaningful as part of a fulfilled, complete life. Be sure you maintain a balance and don't let others rope you into taking on tasks and work that aren't your responsibility. Be careful if someone is constantly trying to gain access to your emotional world and is showering you with statements about their emotions. It's important for you to maintain control over your emotions - don't let someone else take this control away from you! You should also try to not always repress your own feelings. This will make you less susceptible to others' attempts to manipulate you.

11. How to manipulate an Aquarius

Aquarians are the rebels of the zodiac world. They are continuously up in arms against standards and authorities, attempting to change the world and make it better. They feel at home when confronting problems and ideas on an intellectual level. In the course of the seasons, they represent a time in which winter still reigns, but the days are already getting longer. The cycle of life has turned the corner from death towards life. Awakening, new beginnings, and change are dominant topics in the lives of people with the zodiac sign Aquarius. Freedom and independence are very important to Aquarians, as they need these to express themselves. They also value a large circle of friends, although they do not develop extremely intense relationships with individual people.

They will never have just one best friend, but will always be surrounded by multiple friends or a clique. Aquarians are deeply interested in life and in other people; they want to learn about and understand everything, and won't reject any experience. They are characterized by an easy-going nature that makes them popular without having to work for popularity. They seek answers in spirituality but, as in many areas of their lives, remain eternal seekers. On the negative side, Aquarians can be eccentric and cold, and their views can be quite radical.

There are multiple ways to manipulate an Aquarian. One way is to isolate them from their friends and networks. Aries, Aquarius' third sign, follows this approach by spreading rumors about the Aquarian and his friends and destroying his friendships. Leos can outshine Aquarians through loud self-promotion and dominate Aquarians around their friends. One other option for Leos is engaging Aquarians in loud arguments that are overheard by others. Aquarians shy away from such situations.

Aquarians hate feeling boxed in or making compromises. Because of this, they are susceptible to manipulation by Cancers, who can blackmail them emotionally and force them into making concessions. Aquarians aren't quarrelsome. They don't have a thick skin, and often wear their hearts on their sleeves. People with the zodiac sign Taurus can convince them they're egotists and don't worry about their family enough or don't respect traditional and conservative views. Libras pretend to be interested in an Aquarian's large number of ideas and projects, tricking them to gain their trust. Pisces appeal to the Aquarian's sympathy and humanity and pretend to need their help. This manipulation won't succeed for very long, since the

Aquarian's need for freedom is so great, but it can succeed for a short time.

Capricorns can make Aquarians feel inadequate by convincing them that although they have plenty of good ideas, they lack the strength to implement them successfully. Virgos have the greatest manipulative influence on Aquarians. Order, continuity, and reliability are not an Aquarian's strengths. Virgos can organize many important aspects of everyday life for them, making themselves so indispensible that they eventually take over complete control of the Aquarian's life. The Aquarian only needs to experience a supposed or actual life crisis, and the door is open wide for Virgo's manipulation.

Sagittarians will help Aquarians out with money if they're in a pinch again, but will expect copious thanks and favors in return. One Aquarian can manipulate another by poisoning his environment with disparaging remarks.

A Gemini, on the other hand, will steal some of an Aquarian's numerous ideas and portray them as his own. Anyone who wants to manipulate an Aquarian will do so easily by pretending to be like-minded with him. Common interests and hobbies, or working together on a project, provide good opportunities. Aquarians are quick to approach other people, and are skilled at bringing people together. Due to their deep understanding of others and sense of philanthropy, they are also more than willing to help others for free, even if they don't provide this help for a long period of time, and even if reliability is not one of their strong suits.

An Aquarian's need for freedom does, however, make it difficult to manipulate him for very long. His large circle of friends stops one person from having too much influence over him, which is why isolation is such an important step in manipulation.

If your zodiac sign is Aquarius, you should be vigilant if someone continuously tries to separate you from your friends, either through rumors or through feigned neediness. Don't let yourself get caught up in emotional blackmail, and whatever you do, protect your freedom.

It is important for you to take on responsibilities in your life instead of relinquishing these to others, since this is a major gateway to manipulation. No matter how unpleasant you find these everyday tasks, you should never give them over to others who might have ulterior motives. This is especially true in a crisis situation, be it simply a broken bone or something as major as a lost job.

12. How to manipulate a Pisces

Pisces are the last zodiac sign in the calendar. They represent the time starting at the end of February, when it is still cold, but the beginnings of spring are palpable. Everything is in the act of becoming, the world is hidden, and buds and leaves are waiting underground. Nothing is certain, everything seems to be sleeping and dreaming of future possibilities without the need to be tied down. This also describes the nature of a Pisces. They are dreamers, closed-off people who are more likely to be engaged in a dream world than anchored in reality.

They don't like to make commitments, remain in the abstract, and are controlled more by feelings than rational considerations. They possess a great longing for love, bliss, and fulfillment, making them susceptible to abusive relationships and a variety of addictions. They don't like to go against the flow, quickly react in an offended or hurt way, and are good-natured and benevolent. Pisces thrive on inspiration, and often inspire others to create art. Spirituality and art play an important role in their lives.

The 12th house, which they represent, stands for transcendence, cosmic consciousness, spirituality, and dreams. Pisces seek out inner truth, and are full of compassion for other creatures. Both of these aspects make them susceptible to manipulation.

Libra has the greatest manipulative effect on people with the zodiac sign Pisces, as the eighth sign. Pisces can't handle crises and setbacks well. They lack energy, decisiveness, and the courage to make choices, which they need to deal with these kinds of challenges. Instead, they withdraw, become addicted to daydreaming or substances, and forget reality. A Libra can take advantage of this condition by influencing a Pisces to make bad decisions. They could be attempting to push the Pisces into emotional dependency, or just to manipulate them in general. Pisces easily lose their inner compass, leaving them helpless. Libras can cause them to believe they are taking over leadership responsibilities, plunging them into misfortune.

An Aries will use a Pisces lack of skill in handling money to buy them with expensive gifts or loans, while a Gemini will try and convince them not to rely on their much-touted gut feelings.

Pisces, similar to Cancers, make decisions from the gut. However, it is difficult for them to make clear decisions, and they are often hesitant and have a hard time making commitments. They usually keep an escape hatch open somewhere. Scorpio can attack here, by declaring this behavior as cowardly and hypocritical and maligning the Pisces in front of others.

Leos can force Pisces into too many concessions to reality, which will make the Pisces unhappy. They need their dream world to feel complete and at home.

Virgos take a similar approach by talking Pisces out of this dream world and forcing them to accept large numbers of obligations. Saying "no" isn't a strength Pisces have, making it easy to get them to do things they don't actually want to do.

Cancers, on the other hand, will reinforce the Pisces tendency to flee from reality, which can cause serious difficulties for them. They can entice them to consume alcohol and drugs and keep them from fulfilling their duties.

Capricorns can also use the Pisces' tendency to daydream for themselves, by painting reality as highly negative and making Pisces feel as though they're too weak and unstable for this world.

Aquarians, on the other hand, will desecrate everything important to the Pisces using biting or insulting comments, while Sagittarians will constantly threaten to leave Pisces, which is a way to blackmail them. They will offer themselves up as protectors, simultaneously fulfilling two of Pisces longings: the longing or a protector, and the longing for love.

The Pisces' inconstant character makes it relatively easy to influence them. It's not in their nature to be tied down to reality. However, this means that a manipulation may not have a very strong or long-lasting effect. Pisces are highly emotional people who have a difficult time differentiating themselves from others. They experience others' sufferings as though they were their own. This great compassion is another way for others to influence them.

As a Pisces, it is important for you to maintain your contact with reality and to seek out people who can balance you and ground you, and who are trustworthy. You should always be cautious if someone attempts to encourage you to use drugs, alcohol, or other addictive behavior to escape reality. Dreams and inspiration are important, but they're just one aspect of life - you need to experience other aspects as well. Your deep need to be loved makes it easy for others to manipulate you, as does your desire to be protected. Love should never come with conditions. The search for a protector is a childish way to escape reality, and stops you from leading a happy adult life.

Closing Remarks

The twelve relationships we've described here, and their potential for manipulation, have not simply been placed in random order. These twelve types of encounters between the zodiac signs also symbolize the twelve central time periods in your life, during which you are manipulated in various ways. These phases don't just correspond with the chronological sequence of early childhood, youth, adolescence, middle age, and end of life - instead, we experience them again and again, any time our lives force us to make a change and reinvent ourselves. How strongly the manipulation will affect you isn't just a question of which zodiac signs are combined, but also depends on the life situation in which you currently find yourself.

You pass through a phase of self-discovery in the earliest years of your life. Just as a small child doesn't yet understand his own identity, this phase is marked by a search for oneself and by facing all kinds of illusions. We are not manipulated by others during this phase, but rather by ourselves. Before we can act, we must first determine who we are and who we want to be. These are the kinds of questions one asks oneself, for instance, after a divorce, a serious illness, or a career change

Self-understanding becomes action during the second phase, although this remains an action focused purely on material concerns and on ensuring one's continued existence. A typical question in this phase might be: "What must I do to ensure my livelihood and that of my family?" We do not contemplate for long in this phase; instead, we simply do what is necessary. At the same time, this phase is also characterized by independence. We are no longer dependent on the help or care of others. The phase is symbolized by a child who is no longer dependent on his mother, but can instead do many things on his own.

Pressing existential questions are answered during the third phase, providing space for new ideas and for interaction with others. New, interesting people come into our lives, bringing new ideas and worldviews and enriching our worlds. We feel that establishing contact with others and finding opportunities to express ourselves are necessary ways to enrich our lives. We might imagine this phase as an engaged student. The danger of being manipulated in this type of phase is very high.

A certain disillusionment takes place in the fourth phase. Experience has shown that not all encounters are positive, but rather that there are other people in the world who are ready to hurt and manipulate us. We reflect on what is past and what is familiar, as well as our backgrounds and friends, and miss the past. We are even ready to idealize that which we turned away from during the first phase. This is a time of concessions, like those we typically experience from our mid-20s. Withdrawal can often keep us from being exposed to manipulation.

The fifth section describes that phase of life when children slowly become older and one once again has times for one's own ideas and projects. This is a phase of creativity and breakthroughs which thrive off of experiences we have had. The enthusiasm of the third phase is gone, as well as the disappointment we still felt in the fourth phase. Instead, these have grown into an understanding of how to accept and enjoy life in all its aspects. The danger of manipulation increases again in this phase, for creativity requires inspiration and interaction with others.

The fifth phase is followed by the sixth, in which creativity wanes and we return to the questions of everyday existence. We do not search for affirmation in art or new projects, and our large numbers of contacts can be depleted. Instead, we seek out comfort. This can also be a phase in which all of the small problems of everyday life, such as a tax form we haven't filled out or an incorrect invoice can seem to blow up around us, destroying all our creativity.

During the seventh phase, we turn outwards once again. This turn is often part of a search for a partner, with many middle-aged people making a second attempt to find happiness. The play of attraction and desire offers many opportunities for manipulation, so a high level of mindfulness is prudent in this phase. This is difficult however, since anyone who wants to love and be loved also wants to trust, not watch out for potential manipulation.

The eighth phase must follow the seventh. It represents separation, crisis, illness, and loss. At the same time, it symbolizes a chance at transformation and rebirth, and the strength to resurrect oneself anew from the rubble. This is the time when the danger of manipulation is at its greatest. Everything seems to be out of joint, and it is easy to be influenced.

The ninth phase reflects what we have experienced before. It is focused on central questions of worldview, such as "Why am I here?" "Is there a God?" or "Why is this happening to me?" Manipulation is possible in this phase, too, a time when you may be enticed by all sorts of charlatans and gurus. At the same time, however, in this phase we are able to see through the many manipulations we've experienced before and analyze these. During the tenth phase of life, existential questions become meaningful once again. In this phase, we look back on what we have achieved in life and what social position we occupy. The last phase of life is often marked by a somber confrontation with reality. Manipulation is difficult in this time.

It is, however, possible to experience another two life phases. The first of these is the eleventh section, which is characterized by freedom and friendship. All battles have been fought, there is no longer anything to win or lose, and we enjoy every day. The last phase deals with dreams, hallucinations, and turning away from this world in order to pass over to the next. This process usually takes place apart from others and within ourselves, but manipulation nevertheless takes place very often here.

I hope that you have recognized your own experiences in many sections of this book, and share my amazement at how easy it is to manipulate people based on their zodiac signs. Understanding this possibility is the first and most important step to confronting this manipulation. Carefully analyze your environment to discover whether there is someone around you engaging in the type of manipulation described here, and make certain this person no longer has any influence over your life.

Printed in Great Britain
by Amazon